Surprise Was My Teacher

$\mathscr{M}$emories and Confessions
of a Television Producer/Director Who Came of Age
During Television's Adolescence

MERRILL BROCKWAY

SUNSTONE
PRESS

SANTA FE

Sunstone books may be purchased for educational, business, or sales promotional use. For information please write: Special Markets Department, Sunstone Press, P.O. Box 2321, Santa Fe, New Mexico 87504-2321.

Book and Cover design ▸ Vicki Ahl
Body typeface ▸ Californian FB
Printed on acid free paper

Library of Congress Cataloging-in-Publication Data

Brockway, Merrill.
 Surprise was my teacher : memories and confessions of a television producer/director who came of age during television's adolescence / by Merrill Brockway.
   p. cm.
 ISBN 978-0-86534-748-9 (softcover : alk. paper)
 1. Brockway, Merrill. 2. Television producers and directors--United States--Biography. I. Title.
 PN1992.4.B76A3 2010
 791.4502'33092--dc22
 [B]
                        2010002600

Published in

WWW.SUNSTONEPRESS.COM
SUNSTONE PRESS / POST OFFICE BOX 2321 / SANTA FE, NM 87504-2321 /USA
(505) 988-4418 / ORDERS ONLY (800) 243-5644 / FAX (505) 988-1025

The signal for writing my memories was my adult recognition of how deeply I loved my father. We were together not long enough, but his love and trust instilled and encouraged my self-confidence. That prepared me for what was to come in my life.

My deepest appreciation to:

ℰric Roybal, who tutored me in the complexities and rewards of using a computer and how to avoid vexations. This prepared me for the journey to write my memories and Tom Maguire, who edited the finished text, advised me, and prepared it for publication.

These two friends were invaluable in writing *Memories and Confessions*.

Additionally, I am grateful to those generous colleagues (whom you will read about in the text), who developed and sharpened my artistic awareness.

Prelude

On the morning of 27 September, 2007 I struggled out of bed before 7AM with my mind ready to write my memories; the decision had been forming during the night. Eric, our two Scotties, Max and Minnie and I were spending a month at the ocean in Oceanside, California. The sound of the waves was a perfect accompaniment to writing.

The idea of writing my memories had passed through my mind periodically with plus and minus reactions. When a few friends and colleagues had suggested it, I always said, "We have enough of those books." Apparently, I quietly and unconsciously began to reconsider.

I was in my eighty-fifth year; the confirming date would be 28 February, 2008. Regularly, I have been receiving gathering evidence of old age: balance lost, walking difficult and diminishing short term memory, an experience that is shared by all past sixty and, in some cases moved down to fifty. Fortunately, I remember the significant signposts of my growing up and maturing. I never kept a diary; so I don't carry that kind of baggage. I just have trouble with what I said five minutes ago; don't bother with yesterday. My cousin, Betty, has a response to a question you ask her, "How soon do you need to know?"

My intention was not to write my memories for publication; sensationalism seekers will not find any. I would like these memories as clarification, explanation and added information for loyal and supportive friends.

I decided to confer with a Santa Fe friend, formerly of Louisville and a writer I respect, Sally Bingham. I read her memories and told her I was overwhelmed by the detail she had remembered of her early years. She laughed and said, "I kept a diary from the age of four." That was no help.

I remembered Agnes de Mille, dancer, choreographer and writer who became, in her late life, my video subject and friend. Her story will appear later, but during our period of working together she told me about her decision to write her memories: "In the war, I wrote my husband, my bridegroom. I was writing and writing and writing, because it was my only thread of life between him and me. And then I saw him at the end of war and got pregnant. I had to sit home and behave myself. I thought, I'll just write my memories. Everybody else is. Why not I? Well, I'd read Isadora Duncan's autobiography. It was an epoch-making book and I didn't think I could rival that, but I had an interesting life too. Sexually, I couldn't compete."

That liberated me. I had no celebrity sexual incidents to reveal, but I've had a life full of surprises. I've met and worked with many compelling people and I've visited fascinating places; so here we are at the beginning.

What to call it was not easy: I didn't want anything pretentious or cute, so I decided to be straightforward and call it **Memories**. After more thought I decided to add **and Confessions**. After all, people my age are too old to hold secrets.

First Years: 1923—1942

$\mathcal{M}$y first memory of being alive was feeling the warmth from a potbellied stove next to me. Two tall people, hovering over me, explained that I was recovering from a childhood illness; that I was lying on a daybed in my grandmother's dining room; and that I was four years old. I also learned that these tall people were called adults and were my parents, destined to be the guiding forces in my early life.

My mother was a demure young lady from a socially conservative, churchgoing family. Her name was Lissa, called Lissie, with a twin sister, Lydia, an older brother and a younger sister. My father was named Howard, called Hob, with a traveling salesman father, who died before I could appear in his life, a dead mother and a brother, Merrill, also dead, but whose name I inherited. My middle name, La Monte, was never explained to me; except that they wanted it to start with L, again in memory of my uncle Merrill's middle name, Loomis. That's a lot to load on a newborn.

My father was the headliner of everybody's—young and old—most-popular list. He was warm-hearted, oozed sex and charisma and he made them laugh. I suspect that my mother was a virgin, sexually needy and attracted to my father's desirability. After all, he was an early twenties, always-horny male. The determined lass anchored the unruly lad. I know nothing about their courtship, but they married in a double wedding ceremony with twin sister, Lydia and her chosen, Guy, eight months later. I was born in 1923.

I do not believe their marriage was made in the stars. I was a creature formed from irreconcilable points of view and incompatible bloodlines.

I was an eight-plus-pound baby and my mother was less than a 100-pound lady. My birth was punishing to her body. That cancelled any plans for a sister to be called Helen.

My father was physically affectionate with me. I'm told that he loved to play with me and that I liked it a lot. One time at a lake, when he tossed me in the air, he missed catching me and I landed in the water, which was the beginning of my primal fear of water that lasted until the army. Of course, I didn't remember that, because I was a baby. I do remember how he didn't expect me to be a baseball player or sports enthusiast, as he was—although I shared a childhood enthusiasm for the Chicago Cubs with him.

I remember nights when my mother was not at home and I was lying in my bed in my room—the size of a small closet—my father would turn out all lights and play the trombone, slowly walking throughout the house. The music would get louder then softer. He played soulful, improvised music, yearning music. It sounded mysterious. It scared me; yet it thrilled and excited me.

All this happened in our first home where I was born in my parent's bedroom. It was called the little house, and it indeed was. It was there that my lifetime passion for music began when I was seven. An unexpected piano arrived from my grandmother's parlor. My father sat on the piano bench and initiated me into the mysteries and complexities of music. He was willing, natively musical, but untrained. My father was my first mentor.

The little house did not have an indoor toilet. The outside toilet was a short distance from the kitchen door; passage was hot in the summer and freezing in the winter. On Halloween the town's youthful pranksters annually tipped it over sometime during the night. My father roared his anger—then never did anything. Finally, he had a plan: he would sit inside the outhouse and head 'em off at the pass.

It started on script, but later he either dozed or they approached without sound; whatever, they tipped it over with him inside and made a lightning getaway. My father rushed into the house and immediately began making plans and soon we had an inside toilet.

My mother was another pot of tea. She was not physically affectionate at all. Years later I asked about her physical reserve; her reply was, "I grew up without hugging; my father never hugged me." I didn't know how to unscramble that.

I talked about it with my cousin Betty, the daughter of the other twin. Her observation was the same as mine: "They were proud of us but unable to give physical affection, so they substituted presents. Your mother knew you liked peanut brittle; so she sent it to you in Philadelphia and New York. My mother sewed; so she made dresses for me—usually too large." I also asked her daughter, Claudia, for her remembrances of my mother: "serious, nice, proper, held in, meticulous, jealous of her sister." And, I might add, controlling.

Lissie had her own ideas on how one must look and behave in proper society. She was developing her rules and becoming a control artist. And, she was developing them on me; I was to be her first example of excellence. She had ideas about my clothes, my hair, my manner—and she explained them to me, without raising her voice and I did as she wished. My mother formed the rules of behavior I grew up with. They were strong and unrelenting; I obeyed them. I didn't know any different; I was unformed.

I was told later that a child either rebels or gives in. Curious, the idea of rebelling never occurred to me. I remember overhearing my father complaining, "You're making him too neat and his hair is always combed. He's a boy and needs to be free." I believe that was when I began to feel different and disconnected from my peers.

As I was growing up I would edge closer and closer to the subject of sex with my mother. She usually avoided it, but at one point she said, "I never refused your father." For me, that revealed the story.

I believed that my mother planned to guide my father towards her persuasions and restrictions. It didn't work. In the world outside the home my father was cheerful and outgoing; at home he was serious and sensible. When he drank, and he drank more and more rye whiskey and water as I was growing up, he would lash out when being pressed; but there was never any sign of violence.

My most indelible memory from that period is pacing on top of the two feet high wall in front of the little house, first to the east, then to the west, again and again, muttering, "I've got to get out of here." The Great Depression had tuned and was ready to play its mischief. It was impossible to even think about getting out.

We survived that dreadful period because we lived in a small town away from the economic disaster of the large cities. My mother had a large garden and my father made an arrangement to buy and butcher meat from my mother's family farm, now owned by her brother, her father's favorite—after all, he was the oldest of the children and a boy. In those days that was enough qualification.

I remember my father working several jobs: he was a skillful painter of the interior of houses and a refinisher of furniture. He was much sought after. He was the only painter I've ever seen who was ambidextrous; he could paint with both hands at the same time. When we moved into a larger house, he asked me the color I wanted him to paint the walls of my new and roomier bedroom. I told him bottle green and lime. And he did it. I loved being in that room; it was mine.

My father was also a butcher, first class. During my teen years he owned a market in South Bend; his assistant was Mac, an elder gentleman. One summer my parents drove to California for a vacation. I was glad I was not included because our car was a two-seater with a rumble seat, an uncovered folding seat in the rear of the car, open to the elements. And that would have been my place. My father surprised me by leaving me in charge of the market with Mac to help me. I knew nothing about a meat market, but Mac did and he ran the business while I manned the cash register.

Later my father went back to the home improvement and decorating business as a salesman. During the Great Depression we lived on his pay of $15 a week.

My father was always proud of any of my school accomplishments and he was especially proud when, in my teen years, I began to win piano contests. If my mother felt any pride in me; or what I did, she never spoke about it.

As I was writing this, a wave of feeling in my lower depths, rising slowly, began to surface, remembering my mother. It is an intense feeling of resentment, which has been within me, lying silently and ignored for eighty years.

Recently, I talked with my friend Danny Stadler, who lived with me while he was a student at Columbia. He said, "That's not true. You've been angry about this as long as I've known you." Such is the reliability of memory.

When I was fifteen, a group of my friends gathered on our screened-in porch. At a point my mother walked in, surveyed the situation, saw that I was smoking and said, "Oh, I see that you've added smoking to your many accomplishments." In those days smoking was *de rigueur*, the younger the better.

Then, several vivid memories from middle life:

Years later while I was living in New York; I would fly to visit my mother in Indiana. One time, during my long hair hippy period, I showered and visited her in the kitchen while combing and drying my hair. We talked and she said, "Your hair makes you look like an old woman." Later, she added, "Your wrinkles make you look so old." I thought: you sure know how to hurt a fellow, but I said nothing.

I returned to New York. Then, for the first time, I determined, "I'm not going to let her get away with it." So, I returned to Indiana and made her a candlelight and wine dinner. Near the end I said, "I don't think it's any surprise that soon I'm going to be fifty. It's not forbidden, illegal, or immoral. Everybody gets to do it—if they're lucky. If that is going to make you uncomfortable (long pause)—I won't be able to see you anymore. Silence for evermore about my wrinkles."

Growing up, I would have been bereft without the presence of my maternal grandmother. It was to the warmth of her potbellied stove that I woke up. She had three grandchildren, but it was common gossip that I was her favorite, because I was the first born, on her fiftieth birthday.

During this growing up period my mother often worked and I would be in the care of my grandmother. She was a churchgoer who liked to sing hymns. She had a favorite rocking chair and I liked to sit below, wrap her wide skirts and apron around me and feel warm and protected. Then, she sang, usually the hymn *The Old Rugged Cross*, her favorite. It was not a soothing sound to a musical ear; so I would peek out and emphatically say, "Gramma, don't sing."

My grandmother was my morals and ethics teacher; at least I thought so, until later at Columbia College, a professor would explain them to me: Morals are about your relationship with your God; ethics are about your relationships with your fellow men. That last one was her triumph. She taught it with her life. She told me about respect for yourself and others, to live your life wisely and let others live theirs, to seek your own privacy and respect other's privacy (although she was discombobulated once, when she found me sleeping naked on her screened-in sleeping porch).

The last years of her life were spent at a retirement home. When she was going to be one hundred years old, of course I wanted to be there and I flew from New York. My mother met me at the airport and drove me to the home. She said, "She has been asking when you would get here." We arrived and I was pleased to see so many people had come to honor her. I was eager to talk with her when my mother said, "Perhaps, you shouldn't go to her; you're fifty years old and she'll be expecting to see a young boy." I had always done my mother's bidding and I did it again. I was a wuss, an automaton. What prompted her to do that to her own mother and to her only son? And, what prompted her only son, an adult, to obey?

The town where all of this happened was New Carlisle, a northern

Indiana town of 800 people. It was equidistant between South Bend (University of Notre Dame, Singer Sewing Machines and Studebaker autos) and La Porte (Allis Chalmers Farm Machinery). I grew up believing that fabled Route 66 distinguished the town by running through it. Later, much later, I was reminded that New Carlisle lies east of Chicago and that Route 66 begins in Chicago and runs west. So much for distinction.

The town's church-going population was entirely Protestant of various persuasions, each with its own church. There was a whiff of Catholicism, but only on the outskirts of town. I never knew where that church was and I didn't know about Jews until my pre-teens when I visited nearby Hudson Lake and was told that Jews from Chicago were vacationing there.

New Carlisle's political situation was unanimously Republican. My father was one of the table-pounding zealots; in fact, he ran for the office of County Commissioner, but the party bosses and the electorate did not favor him. I remember a few class members and I made signs for the windows of local businesses, mine was the barbershop: "VOTE FOR HOOVER." That surely was 1932. As Judge Judy says, "The apple doesn't fall far from the tree." In 1940 my father drove me south to Seymour, Indiana to see and hear Wendell Willkie accept the nomination as the Republican challenger to Franklin D. Roosevelt's third term. I had no opinion, but there was a lot of cheering. He was the first national politician I had ever seen.

By the time I was ready for school, happily, our new house was across the highway from the school. The event of my first grade was a crush I had on a classmate, Maxine. I gave her a ring—and she lost it. I was embarrassed, but I reported the truth and that generated much conversation and laughter at the dinner table.

In the third grade I had a defining moment. I won a chalk-drawing contest. I didn't regard it as much; since I had copied the subject, but my teacher did: she invited my mother and me to meet in her classroom. As they talked, outside voices became louder and began to distract. My teacher asked me to close the open door on the far side of a closet. I went, but before I closed the door, I looked into a locker room and saw the older boys basketball team. I saw naked adolescent boys. At that moment, the question of my sexual preference was settled. I was eight years old.

In the fourth grade my education began. The teacher was Mary Cauble and she taught grammar—and did she ever. I have continued to remember and use her teachings, including those that have gone out of style: Mary said, "You raise animals, but you rear children." I know I'll never win that one and when did "graduate from college" become "graduate college?" If she were alive today, she would say that the language has become unspecific and lazy and our conversations have followed suit.

In the fifth grade I had Papa Clyde who loved literature and lured me into loving literature. The next year I had a man with a gold tooth and a pedantic teaching technique who tried to interest me in history. He was boring. I don't even remember the area of history he was teaching.

From the beginning of school I was a good student, I worked hard and I got the best grades, but I was a lonely child, a different child. It would take many more years to learn how to be alone but not lonely.

After my discovery of the naked boys in the third grade, I knew this preference was not acceptable in this town, in this state, in this country. The only choice was silence, the closet. It wasn't until an accepting college, Columbia, and an accepting city, New York, could I begin to peek out.

I have a friend, a lawyer in Indianapolis, who writes a periodic column in the local newspaper. She sends them to me. I quote from a recent column:

"I can't imagine living your entire life in fear that someone will figure out that you aren't who you pretend to be. Just think of the amount of energy it must take to erect and maintain that sort of facade—energy that might be devoted to more productive and enjoyable ends."

Near the end of my eleventh grade my algebra teacher asked me, in class, about my grades, which he already knew. I acknowledged that in every grading period since the first grade, I had received an A. That sparked my thinking and I went to my parents and said, "I would like to get a better education: more challenges, more opportunities in my senior year." I wanted to go to La Porte, which my investigation had told me was a better high school than South Bend. My parents supported my wish, but explained that money or the lack of it was the obstacle. Lissie—who had been known to pin $5 bills behind draperies and under rugs "just in case," saved the day. Her gutsiness and ingenuity burst forth. She arranged rides to and from La Porte, stay-overs when necessary, plus modest pocket money. This, truly, was the first time I felt that my mother was thinking of me and not her plan for me.

La Porte High School was a most fulfilling experience. I was exposed to much of what I had been deprived of—especially debate—and the spirit and the enthusiasm encouraged my development. I graduated as the Salutatorian. Katie Howes was the Valedictorian and she deserved it because she had been there from the beginning. And, she was smart.

I was now a high school graduate. I wanted to go to the University of Chicago where the *Great Books* program was taught. My father said, "The Depression is still sleeping in our house;" so I enrolled at Indiana University, where tuition was free, to study music, especially piano.

Those two years were uneventful, until one day I noticed on the music department's bulletin board an announcement of a recital with a pianist playing his own music. I had never heard of the pianist, Bela Bartok, but I soon would. On stage, he entered; I first saw that he was short and trim, and about sixty years old. His manner was shy and modest. Then he began to play. I was jolted; I had never heard such sounds. I was told that the music was tonal, but it wasn't the tonality I'd ever heard; flashes of familiarity followed by strangeness: dissonant sounds, raucous, shrill, soothing then strident, all with massive energy.

It took me a few days to assemble my thinking facilities: I decided not to be judgmental based on what I already knew, but to explore the world Bartok introduced me to. I learned about his *Microcosmos*, his six-volume piano instruction he wrote for his son, and I took them into my piano practice. My exploration continues today.

I later learned that the university paid Bartok $100 for the recital, and that he died of leukemia, previously undiagnosed, in 1945.

Merrill, the young pianist

I studied piano with Professor Hofzimmer, a student of the famed Busoni. I waited tables in a sorority; joined the Phi Delta Theta fraternity and led their chorus and was temporarily lured out of the closet by a lecherous fraternity brother who later married and had eight children.

Sometime during my growing up period I learned to play bridge, the card game fashionable at that time. At the fraternity an upper classman spotted my bridge skills and suggested that we become partners. On an early December Sunday morning during my first semester, my partner and I were preoccupied in a challenging bridge competition in the fraternity game room, when the radio announced that Japanese planes had bombed far-away Hawaii. Now, no eighteen-year-old small town Indiana boy in his first year of college could possibly intuit how this "day of infamy" would transform his life.

A declaration of war soon followed. Every American male alive at that time was asking: What's going to happen to me? The Enlisted Reserves offered a pill: Take me and you will be able to finish four years of college. I took the pill, but it was a promise from Hell. I did not finish four years of college; I was called into service at the end of my sophomore year.

World War II: 1943—46

After a drunken harangue by my father about the wickedness and villainy of FDR I was delivered to a midnight train from South Bend to Toledo, Ohio, where, on 21 May, 1943, I was inducted into the US army and immediately shipped to Fort Benning, Georgia for infantry basic training. Ask me about those twelve weeks—or were they eight? Almost sixty-five years later neither I, nor any old soldier I asked, could remember. For me, it was one giant, humongous blur. My group of recruits was made up of soft and spongy college kids. The cadre was lean and tough. The training was concentrated, demanding but compassionate. During this radical change of lifestyle, I first heard the mantra that would be Linus' blanket for me: "And this too shall pass away."

At the end of basic training our group was separated and I was shipped to Fordham University in one of New York City's boroughs, the Bronx, where I was attached to a group being trained for Air Force occupation after the defeat of Germany.

The studies were in German area and language. The faculty was made up of knowledgeable civilian teachers; the students were bright and eager to learn. Two semesters later, a bombshell. The program was cancelled. The announcement was brief and the unannounced explanation was simple: the war was escalating and more of the public was becoming incensed that a selected few were tasting educational privilege. I was returned to the infantry at Camp Carson, Colorado Springs, Colorado.

Before leaving New York I again stopped by Columbia College on Manhattan Island. I had visited the campus several times to become acquainted with the school, its facilities and educational opportunities. By this visit, I was already convinced that I wanted to be educated at Columbia College and live in New York City and I applied. At Camp Carson, during one morning's reveille, unexpectedly and quite unexplainably, I was transferred across the camp to the engineers division. That's the way the army worked: speedy, with no explanation.

The field engineer's job was to build bridges and repair highways. Demolition is a tool of the trade. At one explosives exercise I realized that a fella can get hurt. At the same time I was searching for a way out, the chaplain was looking for an assistant. Because I had musical training and because I promised to learn to pump the field organ, I was assigned to the chaplain. They didn't tell me that my further duties were care and maintenance of the jeep: change the oil, check the tire pressure, wash the vehicle, etc.

Within a few months, my unit, the Headquarters Company of the 1149th Engineer Combat Group, a unit of the 13th Corps and the 1st Army, was shipped to Normandy in the European Theater of Operations by way of England. During a short stop there, one of my soldier companions felt compelled to yell to the shore, "We've come to fight your war."

During the sea voyage in a rocking and rolling hammock aboard a tiny troop ship I received a life-changing letter: Columbia College had accepted me as a student; I could begin learning after the end of the war.

The 1149th Group arrived at Omaha Beach, several months after the *Saving Private Ryan* troops launched the invasion of the continent. The tumult was over. The Germans had pulled back; the beachhead was silent as a tomb, but the high hedges of Saint Lo gave sniper opportunity to retreating German soldiers. There were casualties.

The assignment for the engineers was to service the infantry's march east. The journey began. The chaplain had a secret wish and once overseas it slipped out: to be awarded a Purple Heart for service injury and the Congressional Medal of Honor for risk-taking and subsequently to be appointed the Bishop of Benton Harbor, his home congregation in Michigan.

As organ pumper and jeep driver, my duties were to provide music for the field services and to chauffeur the chaplain. During one visit to a military cemetery, while the chaplain was talking the talk and making nice, I wandered the grounds and came upon a large tent filled with piles of unrecognizable objects. Looking closer, I could identify assorted chunks of male body parts. I slipped behind the tent and vomited, which the chaplain, who wandered by, thought was amusing.

Coincidentally, the company clerk was transferred. The company commander urged me to take the job. I was somewhat uncertain—my antenna was wiggling and the message was: the company commander fancies you. I wanted the job, decided to take it and heightened my watchfulness. No incident occurred.

The path of the 1149th Group's journey was projected to be through Belgium, southern Holland and into Germany, entering just before the Roer River. Around Christmas time I took advantage of the holiday lull to drive south to visit a soldier friend. In the late afternoon, the friend's commander advised a return to base; he said that orders had been received from Corps informing units to take special precautions against the enemy using the quiet period for aggressive actions. I obeyed; the night journey, driving alone into the darkness of a thousand midnights and the wrap-around silence, interrupted only by the labored drone of the jeep motor, was terrorizing.

A communiqué to headquarters: "From indications of weather forecast, ground conditions, enemy reconnaissance and the reports of enemy paratroopers dropped, there seemed to be considerable army concentration." There was and it would be remembered as the Battle of the Bulge, a surprise attack by the Germans against thinly held American lines in the Ardennes. Winston Churchill called it the greatest American battle of World War II and the most "terrible, costly battle ever fought by Americans in any war."

One unit reported finding an "1/8 inch cable strung across the roadway about four feet above the ground, connected at ends to fence posts adjacent to an enemy dragon teeth line at each end of road. The cable crossed the road three times." Translated into civilian language that meant "The Germans strung tight wire from one side of the road to the other at the driver's neck height." I remembered my dark journey back to base: I had driven the jeep with the windshield down, the usual driving practice.

The Bulge was a final death spasm by the Nazi war machine, futile and ultimately catastrophic. The American army's journey continued as the engineers kept roads, muddy from spring thaw, passable and removed land mines

My most frightening memories are about trying to sleep in open fields as buzz bombs putt-putted across the night sky. If the putt-putting stopped, my fright accelerated. That was the signal that the bomb would drop. Where? Near? Here?

Occasionally, there was rest and relaxation (R & R) when small groups of men were sent to recreational sites for relief from stress. I remember Biarritz on the Atlantic coast in southern France, Lugano in the Swiss Alps (as close as I could get to a desired visit to Italy) and especially the Nicholas Baillie Jarvie Inn in the Highlands of Scotland during the blooming of the heather.

And then there was the infrequent entertainment; always held in an immense airplane hanger stuffed with thousands of soldiers. Bob Hope didn't appear, but Katherine Cornell did. Not many of the soldiers knew that Miss Cornell was a most respected actress and a great lady of the American theater. Nor did they know about Elizabeth Barrett and Robert Browning and their love story as told in *The Barretts of Wimpole Street*, the play Miss Cornell and her cast brought to the troops. By the end of the performance they knew and they roared their approval.

The mood for Marlene Dietrich's arrival was the noise and madness associated with today's rock concerts. She didn't enter; she didn't walk on; she materialized—a curvaceous angel in a gold lamé gown. The troops went berserk as she slowly and seductively floated downstage center. Her first words—after the din died down—a smoky, "Hello, Boys." Uproar. She waited until they were hoarse before she bantered with them, teasing them with insinuating sex. They whooped. She offered to sing a song. They cheered. "See what the boys in the backroom will have and tell them I'm having the same..." It became a sing-a-long, with loud applause and cheering at the end. In preparation for her next offering a stool appeared, followed by a bow, as in cello and a carpenter's saw. Miss Dietrich lifted her skirt and placed her foot on the stool—she was wearing army boots. The boys were surprised; they giggled. She positioned the handle of the saw against her knee and with the bow she made music. I don't remember the tune; I do remember the soft vibrating woo-woo sound, Heavenly, I called it.

Marshall, my army buddy and an accomplished musician says, "You must be mistaken. You play the musical saw by sitting down, holding the handle of the saw between your legs, bending the saw with your left hand and bowing with your right."

My reply: "Such is the treachery of memory."

The boys were beside themselves: shouting, stomping the ground, beating each other on the back and crying. During the uproar the Goddess disappeared. She was gone but she had given these soldiers what they needed and yearned for most of all: sex and humor. I was screaming too. I was twenty-one and slipping away from my mother's proper training and I wasn't even embarrassed. I was away from home, homesick and horny, just like the other boys. Besides, I'd never seen a real movie star.

Now, a few words about sex in the army: my bunkmates were my age and I would wager they were as horny as I was; but we were not making do with each other and testosterone was not promising to explode. Was it saltpetre? That was the rumor. I later looked it up and found no explanation other than it was potassium nitrate. My buddies and I determined that it was being put in our food to stop any sexual urges. Whatever it was, it did the job.

By early on February 15th the Germans had been driven back and the 1149th Group had passed through southern Holland and entered Germany on the way to the Roer River. A report stated that heavy equipment could not cross the river, due to enemy destruction of the bridges. The engineers responded with pontoon and Bailey bridges and the infantry was across and headed to the Rhine River. The action accelerated; it was called Operation Grenade.

Sometimes, the battle line didn't move forward neatly; often it was like a glove, allied troops as the fingertips and Germans in between. One day I arrived at the forward location and the Colonel was sitting on a stump looking like the caption of the famous Steig drawing: "People are no damned good." The Colonel and the command company had arrived, but the ammunition hadn't. The Rhine was crossed; Onward to the Elbe.

On our march the 1149th Group opened labor camps in our path. We had not heard that first one, then two inmates had escaped from the Auschwitz death camp to Czechoslovakia and told about the concentration camps and Hitler's "Final Solution". At one labor camp a Russian woman who had given birth the day before, was now released and forced to work in the fields and I remember vividly German bodies swimming the Elbe, away from the Russians toward the allies.

I had entered France as a corporal. In the field, especially when the army is on the move, events often happen unexpectedly and responses must be quick and decisions sharp and to the point. Some time between the Roer and the Rhine I was promoted to Sergeant Major, the highest-ranking enlisted man, carrying the rank of Master Sergeant. I was also the proud bearer of a Bronze Star, for what, I don't remember.

I was the head of Administration: a G1. My best friend, Bob, was the head of supplies, a G4. We were the same age, twenty-two, but looked middle teenage. On one occasion the Colonel, the Boss, was annoyed and told us to call in the field sergeants for a meeting and said, "I want you to chew their asses." We sent out the word; they came, looking unshaven and un-bathed, just like Ernie Pyle's Willie and Joe. Bob and I introduced ourselves and our mission. One bold fella in the back muttered, "Well, I'll be dipped in sh__!" We never found out how effective our chewing-out had been.

Merrill in uniform during World War II

On 25 April, 1945, Soviet and American troops linked up, cutting Germany in two; following that, Mussolini was captured, executed and his body was taken to Milan and hung upside down in front of a gasoline station; Hitler committed suicide in his bunker and German forces surrendered in Italy, Berlin, Northwest Germany, Denmark and Holland. At 2:41 on the morning of 7 May, 1945, the Chief-of-Staff of the German Armed Forces High Command signed the unconditional surrender of all German Forces to the Allies. News of the surrender broke in the West on 8 May, 1945.

Then there was the matter of the reluctant Japanese. Nuclear events at Hiroshima and Nagasaki were convincing. The Japanese understood Truman's presentation. But, the argument to-do-or-not-to-do continues today: Morality or public policy, or perhaps, how humans behave toward each other, even under unusual and extraordinary situations.

Victory on both fronts did not mean that I was immediately dispatched home and discharged; a release point system was operative and I must wait my turn. That included a detour south and an assignment to the eccentric and unpredictable General Patton and his occupation forces. A chronicle of that assignment would take more unpleasant memories than I choose to dredge up.

Finally, in early April of 1946, I was returned to the USA without event. I was discharged at Camp Atterbury, Indiana after thirty-five months of service, which entitled me, according to the GI Bill, to thirty-five months of college education.

Hello Columbia College!
I never learned if the chaplain received a Purple Heart and became the Bishop of Benton Harbor, nor did I care.

COLUMBIA AND BEYOND: 1946—1953

*C*olumbia College in the fall of 1946 was paradise revealed—at least that's what I reported. The entering freshmen, confident of their mastery of book learning, were the superior students of their high schools. Also entering at the same level were the returning soldiers, at least three years older, who brought back war learning. This group had no patience with the undergraduate foolishness that once characterized life in an Ivy League school. The exchanges between the groups were spirited, informed and sustained. They taught each other.

The centerpiece of the Columbia curriculum consisted of two courses every freshman and sophomore was required to take, no matter what he (it was an all male school then) planned for his specialization: *Humanities* and *Contemporary Civilization*. These courses were designed to acquaint each student with the great classics and the philosophy and history of western civilization. The sociologist Daniel Bell claimed, "These courses shocked students into a new appreciation of the dimension of thought and feeling." And, these classes were not taught in lecture halls by teaching assistants. The classrooms were small and mostly members of the senior faculty presided, seminar style. My most memorable instructor was a professor and the head of the French Department. At that time Columbia's faculty was reputed to be the best of any undergraduate college—or at least we thought so.

To quote Norman Podhoretz, a brilliant schoolmate of mine, who has disappointedly become an intellectual centerpiece of Neocon thinking: "Before Columbia I had never truly understood what an idea was or how the mind could play with it. Before Columbia I had never truly understood that, as an American, I was the product of a tradition, that past ages had been inhabited by people like myself and that the things they had done and the thoughts they had thought bore a direct relation to me and to the world in which I lived."

But it was not all books and study. I had a southern classmate with a passion for baseball and that reinvigorated my memory of the Chicago Cubs and Gabby Hartnett hitting a pennant-winning homerun in the twilight hours. That was in 1938 and I heard it on the radio of an old lady neighbor who was a curmudgeon to everyone but me because we were Cub fans. My southern friend and I bonded for baseball reasons, except this time it was the New York Giants, who didn't move to the west coast till much later. Many afternoons we would subway to the Polo Grounds, drink beer and cheer on the Giants. I witnessed two major homeruns: Willie Mays' first and Bobby Thomson's pennant-winning homer. We both loved to watch the antics of Leo Durocher after his arrival from the archrivals, the Brooklyn Dodgers, before they moved to the West Coast.

A classmate invited me to join him to see "Martha". Martha who? He explained that Martha was the leading pioneer of modern dance. That was foreign territory for me; where I came from it was all waltzing. "Martha even invented her own dance language," he continued. By that time I was becoming curious; so I agreed. We took the cross-town bus to the 92nd Street YMHA for my first experience of modern dance—1946. I saw a tiny lady dancing a solo: she grabbed my gut, swung it around, tossed it in the air, slammed it to the ground, then tenderly picked it up and cradled it. I would be forever Martha Graham's disciple.

Then, there was my classmate and soon-to-become friend from New Jersey and rumored to be from a Mafia-connected family. I never asked; so I never knew. Jimmy Zito had the most brilliant mind, memory and language skills I had ever encountered. But, he couldn't write. My roommate, Willie was a serious editor—that's what he did after we graduated—and he would often help Jimmy to realize his assignments. The scene: Jimmy would arrive at our room, Willie would take his place at the typewriter, and Jimmy would eloquently speak the paper as Willie typed. At the end Willie would check his work, then hand the paper to Jimmy who would accept it and begin to exit. I, who had witnessed the performance, would say, "Don't you see what Willie is doing for you?" His response was, "What? He's only typing what I said;" then he would turn and leave. I truly did not realize the severe consequences of his denying the inevitable.

But then there were fun moments when Jimmy and I would sneak out of the closet and subway down to the bars in Greenwich Village. I was cute and had no problem striking up conversations, but Jimmy was not cute and he was left alone until he began reciting Shakespeare. At that time I believe he knew three Shakespeare plays from memory. And he knew them all from the beginning to the end. He would choose the one he thought most appropriate to the occasion, then begin his performance. The audience was a bit slow at the beginning, by the middle they were becoming more interested and at the end they all wanted Jimmy to go home with them.

Also, I had a job as accompanist at a voice studio in Carnegie Hall. I had never seen or imagined the skills this teacher had. He was not a vocal coach, he was a voice technician who repaired and restored broken voices or expanded the possibilities of healthy ones. I played for several Broadway stars, always actors who wanted to add to their skills. The teacher volunteered to teach me, too. I learned valuable information about the human voice and I further learned that I had no undiscovered vocal talent.

Columbia undergraduate life and learning was over all too soon.

Graduation day was presided over by Dwight Eisenhower who was Columbia's President between the end of World War II in 1945 and his US Presidency in 1952. Jimmy Zito and I, each properly attired in cap and gown and filled with wine, tearfully repositioned our tassels and lamented, "I'm graduating from college and I don't know anything." We both graduated *cum laude*.

There is a follow-up chapter to the Jimmy Zito tale. He had a sure-fire appointment to the Columbia faculty. He had passed his orals illustriously, but he didn't write his thesis, not because he was lazy or wouldn't—he couldn't; he had writer's block—and he was too proud to talk about it and seek a remedy. Columbia had no alternative but to let him go; the rule was: Write or leave.

Columbia had another rule: to graduate you must pass the swimming test. Ironically Mortimer Adler, the brain behind the *Great Books* concept, didn't pass and didn't graduate. Only decades later did he receive an honorary degree. I passed only by a hair and a whisper, thanks to Jimmy Zito and his diverting conversation with my tester, one of Jimmy's fraternity brothers.

Jimmy was offered and accepted a professorship up the Hudson at Sarah Lawrence. My friend Mary Willis was his student and attests that Jimmy's teaching was eloquent and inspirational. But there's more: apparently, from anonymous reports, he decided to become heterosexual. I never saw or heard from him again. I know he married and had a child. A few years later life turned away from Jimmy and he died. I never learned the cause, but it sounded like a stroke or heart attack.

After I graduated, on the premise of ignorance, I persuaded my faculty adviser to allow me to enroll as a special student, to take courses that would fill the holes in my education; after all, I still had more points from the GI Bill.

That was a rewarding year, but I still had more points; so I enrolled in a two-year course leading to a Masters of Arts degree in Musicology. That was not a good fit. I found out that I was not cut from scholar's cloth; nor could I become a proper professor: tweeds itch and I never could keep a pipe lit. Much to the consternation of the presiding professor of musicological studies I, as best as I could, turned any musicological occasion into a performance. I had begun piano studies again after the war and continued them during my undergraduate and graduate work. I was grudgingly awarded a master's degree—on the condition that I not pursue a PHD. I learned that sometimes you enroll in something and find out that you don't want any part of it. It's a good lesson to be learned. I was lucky that I had the points to learn it.

That was the end of the Columbia years. They were the turning point in my life; they marked the direction and push-started the journey—which continues to this day.

NOTE: I am near finishing my *Memories and Confessions* and now, after careful and extended consideration, I have a confession: the two years I chose to spend in graduate school studying musicology, a subject I deeply didn't like at the beginning, middle or end, was a stupid decision by a willful young man who hadn't thoroughly considered the opportunity. Humanities readings had awakened an interest in history, especially cultural history. I could have pursued that under the guidance of Jacques Barzun, the best of the best. In addition, my reasoning after the fact of a degree was specious.

Following that confession is another confession; this one is my lifetime's greatest embarrassment. The back-story begins at the music department at Indiana University. A classmate was the superbly talented Margaret Hillis with a dilemma: should she be a singer, a pianist, or a conductor? I missed the interlude, but she became the highly praised choral director of the Chicago Symphony during the Solti years, but before that she re-appeared in my life during the early 50s. I had learned Mozart's *Piano Concerto No. 23 in A Major, K488* and she was conducting an orchestra in Brooklyn. She invited me to be the soloist and I agreed. We rehearsed and everything went swimmingly.

The night of the performance arrived; the orchestra played and it was time for my piano entrance and then it happened—I had a complete memory loss. Margaret got through the performance with aplomb and nobody booed, but I have no memory of being a part of it. I do remember my profound embarrassment when I went backstage to see my teacher, who had brought me and his friend Milton Babbitt, the distinguished and highly lauded avant-garde composer.

I remember a tale about Milton: he had written a thesis for an advanced degree from Princeton that was so esoteric that nobody could understand or grade it. Because of my teacher's friendship with Milton I would be in his company regularly. One night at a gathering Milton was playing the piano. I stood by and listened, then asked him, "If you could be any composer, who would it be?" His answer, "Jerome Kern." I didn't have enough wit to ask him why.

During the next three years my life was music: teaching piano, coaching singers, touring as accompanist for celebrated vocal artists and instrumentalists in concert. That played satisfactorily until one night in Salt Lake City. I was sitting in a tub of warm water, relaxing before the evening's recital. Unexpectedly I thought: I don't want to do this anymore. And I didn't. That takes a bit of explaining.

From the age of seven the piano and music had been the focus of my life. From that I learned a lot about myself. In no special order I knew that: I didn't have the technique for a solo career, I no longer felt performance glee, the desire/the need to wow an audience and I had changed from an outside person to an inside person. But, I had learned that I was a good accompanist. I knew my job: how to accommodate the soloist. I had been trained by the best musical mentors and I wanted to ply my skills in other areas of the arts.

Later—many years later, I was privileged to work with and be taught by Balanchine. One of his memorable teachings: "Dancing is not the steps; it's in-between the steps." I think, in the same way: Music is not the notes; it's in-between the notes. I hadn't learned that then. But that didn't resolve my current dilemma: unemployment.

Television and Philadelphia: 1953—1962

By 1950 television was bustin' out all over. I thought that might be worth exploring since, during the summers of my Columbia years, I had been the music/drama counselor in an upscale boys camp in the Adirondacks. I thought, "Perhaps that could be a leg up."

Since I had no television training, I consulted a friend, Kirk Browning, who was in the early stages of what would become a legendary career in television. His advice: "Do it. It's a new field and nobody has any real training. They're doing radio with pictures. You'll take Spinoza to it." That was Kirk's advice.

In 1953 I began the job hunt, but even with Spinoza there was no job in New York. I was advised to "Go to the regions, learn and you'll be brought back." This was not the counsel I wanted to hear. I was, by now, a card-carrying New Yorker who became fidgety and slightly nauseous when I crossed the Hudson. I didn't want to stray too far, so I sent my resume to all television stations as far north as Boston, as far south as

Washington, DC and as far west as Philadelphia. Only one responded and that was Philadelphia, happily, the nearest city to New York.

At that time there was no New York-Los Angeles television because Los Angeles was not in play yet. The networks in New York bought programming from their affiliates. WCAU in Philadelphia was a CBS affiliate owned by a newspaper, the Philadelphia Evening Bulletin and it provided CBS-TV with seven hours of weekly programming. Shortly, WCAU was sold to CBS and became one of its five owned and operated stations.

I was interviewed and hired; the salary offered was $45 a week—take it or leave it. I took it and moved to Philadelphia where a week's pay paid a month's rent on a one room and kitchen apartment above a dry-cleaning shop. WCAU had an innovative training procedure: no matter which department a candidate wanted to join—news, publicity, public affairs, sales, or administration—the training was in production, the heartbeat of television. My first assignment was moving scenery for *Action in the Afternoon*, a daily half-hour western soap opera; broadcast live (this was many years before videotape) from the studio and the adjacent back lot just off Cityline Avenue. I remember that the first day Jack Dolph, my new friend, who was destined to become the Director of CBS Network Sports and I were crouching, during the broadcast, behind scenery we had just positioned. The scenery fell down and we were revealed to the world.

When I worked, I was quite a curiosity because I wore white gloves. I still had concert commitments during the first six months in Philadelphia. Protecting my hands and finding pianos for practice were major concerns.

No training program was being offered or even considered and no staff director had star quality worthy of emulation; so I devised my own training program, which began with nightly sessions in an empty control room in a dark studio. This was for mechanics, to become familiar with the board used for switching from one camera to another. In the early days the director did his own switching. He was also his own technical director, associate director and production assistant. When unions became a presence in production, a technician would switch according to the instructions from the director.

I selected Dwight Hemion for a director model and William Wyler for craft and esthetics. The stylish and inventive work of Hemion illustrated television opportunities. He directed regular series and specials, mostly of a musical nature. Wyler's films, because they were theatrical releases, could be seen less often, but they could be searched out and studied. Wyler was a master storyteller who knew the thrust of each scene and knew how to stage and frame it. From Wyler I learned clarity and simplicity.

Within a year I was promoted to director; then I had the best teachers of all, the cameramen. I was lucky to have especially good cameramen. Just as a choreographer depends on and learns from his dancers, I learned from and depended on my cameramen. If they like you, they teach you; they listen to your ideas and help you to realize them and make them better. I was older than most of my colleagues and had determined what I wanted to do. I knew I couldn't learn by reading books; I could only learn by working with good people. That was a first priority. I further determined that making a lot of money or becoming famous was not high on my priority list.

As a piano student I had learned, after much trial and error, how to practice: how to pull a piece apart and practice the weak sections by themselves. From this experience, it became clear that too many directors rehearse inefficiently. They are forever going back to the beginning and starting over. Many years later Pierre Boulez confirmed my idea. He would have the group play the piece from beginning to end without stopping. "Just go," he'd say, "then we will correct." Along the way he would find out where the problems were and rehearse them. When the weak links were strong, he would put the chain together.

One summer we had a rare opportunity. WCAU was selected by CBS to be the production facility for the *Fred Waring and the Pennsylvanians* show, the summer replacement for *The Garry Moore Show*. It was every weekday morning at 10AM, for half an hour, ninety minutes on Friday, from Shawnee-on-Delaware, Fred's inn in the Poconos. I was assigned to direct. This was my first step out from local directing to the network. There's a different pressure, between local and network productions and I was scared. Fred knew that. He knew when to be tough with me, when to challenge me, when to let me alone, and when to support me—and I got better. I got good enough to be a candidate to direct a full season of *The Garry Moore Show*. But, they decided I was too intense for their purposes.

During our last weeks I received a call that my father had died, felled by his second stroke. During my last visit after his first stroke, I could recognize that he was living in his own private world and that communication was not possible, which saddened me, After I left home we had long periods of separation. I always knew how proud he was of me and how much he encouraged me. Although I was aware that death was not far away, it's arrival was a shock. Fred Waring insisted I go to the funeral, although I couldn't see why, since the person I loved wouldn't be there. He further insisted that I return with my mother. I went and made proper. My mother's accompanying me to Shawnee turned out to be comforting for her. My father was fifty-seven when he died and the year I was fifty-seven was very distressing for me.

My next directorial assignment, one that the other staff directors would argue, plead, threaten or kill to get out of, was the *Horn and Hardart Children's Hour*, an incubator for talented child performers. The issue was the producer; she was ditsy, just like Mrs. Gurney on the old *Wally Peepers Show*.

The program was an hour of skits and songs simulcast every Sunday morning, which meant it was seen on television and heard on radio. The show had a long radio history and the alumni included Kitty Kallen, Eddie Fisher and Frankie Avalon. It was the era of child performers on Broadway and during my assignment eleven of the show's players appeared in Broadway musicals. In directing mostly early- and some later-teens, I made a decision: for me, they were young adults rather than kiddies. Even the kiddies I treated as young adults. I explained what I wanted from them and they responded.

After I extricated myself from *The Children's Hour*, I co-wrote and directed *Kid West*, a western soap-opera with a twist: a traditional storyline with kids riding bicycles and drinking at Miss Magnolia's Sasparilla Bar. The cast included the hero in white (Kid West), the villain in black (Black Eye Dooley) and the slow and dumpy sheriff. The idea didn't make it past the pilot.

I followed that with a weekly series focusing on teen-age accomplishments in the performing arts and called *Expression*. I was able to do that because both Patti Mariano and Dean Stolber, former talented *Children's Hour* performers, had returned from Broadway to graduate from their home schools.

The popular arts were highly publicized. Remember, Rock and Roll started in Philadelphia with Bill Haley and the Comets. But it was also the home of the Curtis Institute of Music, one of the finest conservatories, anywhere. I believed a musical balance was called for. Peter Serkin and Andre Watts were teenage concert pianists in Philadelphia at that time— and there were a surprising number of young musicians, accomplished and waiting to be recognized.

I was the only adult on the show's staff: the production assistants, the writer and the boy and girl hosts, Dean and Patti, all were teens. Patti, had a talented partner, her brother, Bobby, They were the first to go to Broadway in *The Music Man*. Bobby had been one of Liza Minnelli's early boyfriends. He suggested that we invite Liza and his school friend, composer Marvin Hamlisch, to join us in Philadelphia to make an episode of *Expression*. I invited and Liza and Marvin accepted. Liza's mother had dressed her a bit young, so there was scurrying to outfit her properly. The show was one of Liza's earliest, if not first, television appearances.

Patti. Bobby and Dean were also important ingredients in the *Liza and Marvin Show*. Dean had a belting voice and a powerful performing personality. One summer, when he was eight years old, many of the others kids on the *Children's Hour* had gone away on vacation. A few supporting players remained, but Dean's versatility and force of personality saved the shows. Dean was the last to go to Broadway, but when he went, he went big. He was Harvey, a featured role in *Bye, Bye Birdie*, choreographer/director Gower Champion's first Broadway musical.

Dean, as host of *Expression*, talked with the teen-age guests after they performed. I usually wrote questions for him to ask. One day I noticed that he was asking his own questions—and they were more in tune than mine. Afterwards, I asked him, "Where are you going to college?" He said his father wanted him to go to Penn State. My immediate response was, "I think you can do better than that." With the help of a Harvard graduate who worked in the newsroom we organized an application plan and campus visits. After the organized effort Dean was offered full scholarships to six Ivy League schools. He chose Harvard and graduated with his star burnished even brighter. He later went to NYU, became a lawyer and relocated to Los Angeles where he was appointed Vice President of Business Affairs for United Artists. We stayed in touch. Fifty years later when I was preparing the Tennessee Williams video biography, I needed rights clearance for a body of feature film clips. I called Dean for advice. His response was, "I know him; we have lunch every Tuesday;" and "I play tennis with him," and so on. I got permissions for everything I needed.

Patti grew up to be a celebrated character actress, singer and dancer. She's still active on the stage. I lost touch with the writer and the others.

One weekly schedule reported that I was the only director without an assignment; therefore, I would be directing Sunday's *Philadelphia Eagles* football game. The sports fans united and protested mightily. I was invited to join the head honcho in his office. After he closed the door and we sat down, he asked:

Q: Do you go to football games?
A: No
Q: Do you watch football games on television?
A: No

There were several more questions of that nature; finally, I spoke. I pointed out that I would have an experienced camera crew and associate director and that Frank Chirkinian had explained the game to me. Frank Chirkinian was the CBS star sports director; he originated golf on network television. In my early days I had been his assistant.

Frank: "The game is simple. There's a ball and each team wants to get it over the other team's goal line. Neither team wants its goal line crossed so each tries to outwit the other. Simple!"

Q: (not persuaded) Are you sure you're able to do it?

A: Look, I'm not assigned to coach the team. I'm just assigned to direct the broadcast.

He backed off but arranged that I have the best cameramen and the best spotter. On Sunday, during the first play I didn't see the ball, "Hey, fellas, you've done this before, where's the ball?" Soon enough we all learned that it was the hidden ball play. Nobody—spotter, cameramen, let alone me—could find the ball. After that we did just fine. I remember nothing else about that game, including who won and the score.

The last series I directed before leaving Philadelphia—and concurrent with the preparation and recording of the Philadelphia Orchestra—was *Tottle*. It was a project brought to me by Marshall Izen, whom I had met at Camp Carson Colorado's Service Club during World War II. The meetings were not always friendly since we both wanted to show our skills at the piano, usually at the same time. Marshall tracked me down through his cousin who was married to the director of a boy's camp where I was a counselor during the summers of my Columbia years.

Marshall was an enviable pianist. After the war he moved from Chicago to New York to study with the renowned teacher, Madame Vengerova. She was a teacher in the legendary Russian tradition: severe and uncompromising, who would not let her students play anything of their already-learned pieces; rather, only those she assigned. Her reason was: so that they would not regress into their old, bad habits. Marshall left after a year, because he had wider interests—drawing and puppets. But he took with him a splendid piano technique, which was something I never achieved.

Marshall had an idea for a children's program with puppets. We presented it to The Suits (a group that you will hear more about as you read on) and they liked it. Onward and Upward! Then Marshall told me how the idea began—with the last act of the opera *Aida* when Aida joins Rhadames, sentenced to death in an underground tomb. Marshall went home and made a sketch of the scene. Later, Pearl, the wife of a friend, told him about a story she and her fellow child-psychologist, Esther, had written about the incidents within a family. We hired Pearl and Esther and Marshall adapted the story: the family became a mother, father, son and daughter, Coslo and Taffy Tottle, animal puppets who lived in a house below the ground. The comic relief was their friend, Butch Bear. Butch very quickly became my favorite, especially the episode when he went to camp, became homesick and called home. The scene began with laughter, which soon became sobbing. Marshall said it turned into sobbing because he was laughing and couldn't talk. I was in the control room switching cameras when I was overtaken by laughter at Butch's homesick sobbing. I became a patsy for Butch's humor.

Marshall Izen and his set for Tottle.

Marshall designed the extra large puppet set of under-and-above-ground and the scenic department skillfully constructed it. We were joined by two talented young ladies, a fellow puppeteer and a caring producer. Then there was a writer to develop the incidents of Pearl and Esther. The schedule began. Marshall arrived by train from New York at 9.30AM. I met him and we drove to the station to rehearse for a 5PM audio recording session. It was not too long before trouble appeared. I would meet Marshall with the news that we didn't have a script. The reason: the writer began drinking stingers early; at a point he would drink coffee and then the stinger-coffee alternation would continue until he passed out. The solution was that Marshall and I, with help from the ladies, wrote the scripts. We wrote with the help of experiences from our childhoods.

The next problem developed with Pearl and Esther. They were literalists in the most basic sense. They were "from the book", and Marshall and I were writing-out our childhoods, which couldn't be found in their texts. Together we made the decision; they were connected to Marshall; so I remember leaving the room so that he could inform them that their services were no longer required.

Tottle began to attract listeners and win awards, but by that time I was in New York. *Tottle* was a fun period in my life.

The Philadelphia Orchestra was internationally celebrated and had been seen nationally on television. I wanted Philadelphians to see their orchestra televised regularly just for them. To kick it off I devised and later directed, an all-American program conducted by Maestro Eugene Ormandy: Bernstein: *Overture to Candide*; Copland: *Quaker Folk Songs* with William Warfield; MacDowell: *Piano Concerto* with John Browning; Barber: *Adagio for Strings* and Copland: *Tender Land Suite*. The program almost fell apart because of the Bernstein/*Candide*. Ormandy and Bernstein were not fond of each other. They were both conductors of competitive orchestras. Ormandy announced, "The orchestra doesn't know the piece." The assistant conductor was with me and said, "*Au contraire*, maestro, they've played it many times." PAUSE, then Ormandy, "It seems I'm the only one who doesn't know it." He learned it and the show went on.

Merrill (back row, far left) directing the WCAU, Philadelphia production crew in a filming of the Philadelphia Orchestra.

The program was received with enthusiasm and I planned to continue the idea; but the plan was interrupted by an unidentified stranger periodically appearing in the control room when I was directing. After his third visit he introduced himself as the Program Director of WCBS-TV in New York. He invited me to join his staff. I was stunned. I loved Philadelphia; I believed I would never leave. I had a charming apartment housing a Steinway grand on Rittenhouse Square and I drove an Alfa Romeo Sprite. I loved the Friday afternoon concerts of the Philadelphia Orchestra and relished the tryouts of all the important dramas and musicals on their way to Broadway. At the studio I was sitting securely in the catbird seat. I was unsure, but my friends and supporters weren't: "This is an opportunity you cannot refuse." On the afternoon my belongings were being packed and moved, a small group picked me up, took me to dinner and bedded me for the night. Next day they drove me to New York and my new apartment—one arranged by the mothers of Marvin Hamlisch and Patti and Bobby Mariano - just as the movers arrived. I remembered the earlier advice: "Go to the regions, learn and you'll be brought back." After nine years I was a New Yorker again.

A POSTSCRIPT TO THE PHILADELPHIA EXPERIENCE:

     I believe that, in this world, nobody does it alone. I feel especially blessed by supporters: beginning with my badly matched parents who had meager resources, teachers at all levels of my education and especially those men who trained me how to stay alive during the war and, of course, the education from Columbia College and New York City. In Philadelphia, which was the beginning of a new career, I believe I was fortunate to have had a self-appointed mentor, Mel Levine, the assistant General Manager who insisted I learn the basics of my chosen profession: news (I brushed shoulders with Ed Murrow and worked with Walter Cronkite); sports (I actually directed a telecast of a NFL game—to the dismay of the station's sports fans); politics (I met Grace Kelly in her *High Noon* costume, sitting on a camera pedestal waiting to endorse a senatorial candidate whose campaign I was video directing); closed circuit TV (an open-heart bypass operation was especially unnerving) and of course, master control, the central intelligence. To all these assignments I asked the same question:

     Q: "Why do I have to do this?"
     A: "Because you need to know."

New York: 1962

*M*y coming back to New York happened because Dan Gallagher, the Program Director at WCBS-TV, wanted me to work for him. Dan was a big, beefy, red-faced Irish tenor who switched from the chorus of Broadway shows to television because he wanted the world to be filled with art. He believed that television could do just that.

After Dan's third visit to my control room in Philadelphia, he asked me to talk to his staff in New York about a job. I didn't want a job. I had a job. And I loved Philadelphia. But I drove my Alfa Romeo to New York and interviewed three times—reluctantly. Before each occasion I would ask Dan, "What will I be doing?" He was non-committal. After each interview his staff told me "no available job," and they told Dan, "That guy auditioned us." Finally Dan said, "Merrill, don't ask. Just come. I'll find something." And he did.

In the early 60s the CBS-owned stations created a series called *Repertory Workshop*. Dan Gallagher commissioned a piece by Norman Walker, a modern dance choreographer and I directed my first assignment in New York. I directed another; this time it was Paul Taylor and Company dancing his *Aureole*. Both Norman and Paul were loosely derived from Martha Graham—Paul had been in her company and Norman's mentor was May O'Donnell, one of Martha's original dancers—so the language was not foreign to me. Next was a program with Bob Joffrey and Gerry Arpino who were divorcing Rebecca Harkness and forming the Joffrey Ballet. Ballet was a foreign language to me and I floundered. I didn't know what I was doing; I had good intentions and a musical approach, but little else. I determined I must create or find opportunities to learn.

The next assignment was a series of children's specials, including the *Just So Stories* and *Tall Tales*; the latter presented Jack Gilford and a two-man dog, the first Muppet Jim Henson made for television. We had a prime time spot: 5PM Sunday afternoons. That was the former *Omnibus* spot. Audiences connected that time slot with culture till sports programming took over.

Dan also created *Stage 2* for me. That was a monthly, half-hour series of performing arts programs. One Friday in late November 1963—the 22nd, to be specific—I was at a rehearsal studio preparing a program to be taped the following week. I received a call from headquarters to report to the studio ASAP. There I learned that President Kennedy had been shot and had died. CBS was canceling all commercial programming. The alternative was primarily the CBS Orchestra and other related features.

As a director I depended upon preparation. I told them, "I think I can be ready by Sunday." Surprise! A half our later I was sitting in the director's seat. The orchestra and Alfredo Antonini were ready to go and Alfredo had the only scores. Worse, the first piece was the Cesar Franck, *Symphony in D Minor*, whose first movement's principal theme wanders like a butterfly through the instrumental sections—impossible to catch by cameras. I then recognized that there would be no prep time for this assignment. On the spot I had to devise an alternate approach. The agony finally ended—and I wasn't fired.

Stage 2 was broadcast at 8PM, which meant we were out there with the heavy hitters. We did all right for a season. Then, no more; the show was cancelled. I was not challenging to Sid Caesar and Milton Berle.

Next, I was assigned to the documentary film unit. I knew nothing about film or documentary; so I asked if there wasn't something else I could do. The reply was, "Yes, you can find another job." That sobered me and I decided to join the film unit. I didn't know an "A wind" from a "B wind" and for a year the old pros, who did know, worked me over and rolled me around. That was a painful period in my life; my confidence was at low ebb. I learned that old pros are not necessarily the kindest teachers. But I stayed alive and learned the ways film is different from video and I learned the glory of documentary.

Later, the program director (Dan had been promoted) suggested I make a program about the New Jersey High School Orchestra and Chorus. He had been receiving flak from Jerseyites who claimed they were being under-represented. I investigated and reported that I didn't think it was a good idea: "The material is too thin." That was not what he wanted to hear. The suggestion became an unyielding assignment.

The once-a-year event involved young musicians and singers from all over the state. Fortunately I had an ebullient assistant, Rupert Hitzig, a recent graduate from Harvard, whose attitude was, "Of course we can do it." After visits, conversations, thinking and planning, we began filming. The title was *To Make a Joyful Sound*. It was about young people finding their own expression and group togetherness through a musical experience. I drew deeply from my memories of growing up and discovering the joy of making music (I played clarinet in the school band). At that time, some friends said, "It's the best thing you've ever done." Nobody knew that Martha Graham's *Clytemnestra* was in the future.

Rupert and I joined in other projects, but the one I remember most was one CBS initiated for its owned and operated stations: New York, Philadelphia, Chicago, Saint Louis and Los Angeles, The focus was a rash of pregnant teenage marriages across the country in the mid-1960s. Nobody had an explanation; so I was sent to a conference of sociological experts assembled to discuss it. I found that they didn't know anymore than I did; so Rupert and I developed our approach: we titled it, *Marriage!*

A Game for Kids? And our participants would be pregnant teens who married. Now, to find them. Rupert started in Los Angeles and worked east and I started in New York and worked west, both searching, asking for leads and any other way each of us could think of. Rupert was lucky first: the young man who delivered his rental car was a teen husband with a pregnant wife.

We finally found the five couples we needed and began interviews. Our search had convinced us that the situation was not a class issue; all of our subjects were middle class; apparently the other classes had their own ways of dealing with the subject. The couples were forthcoming with their stories and we found a consensus: "We were tired of living at home and being treated like children; we wanted to be treated like adults. We knew that (because of the social conventions of the day) if we got pregnant, our parents would insist that we get married. Then we would be accepted as adults. Then we would be free." I still vividly remember the young mother-to-be who plaintively told us, "I sure hope to meet somebody who knows something about something."

Rupert and I were assigned another project: a series titled *This Is*. Each episode was a half-hour conversation with a preeminent man or woman. The first subject was the architect, Philip Johnson. I was not yet confident about doing conversations and interviews so I hired Jane Kramer, a young writer, whose work for the *Village Voice* I admired. Later she would become a staff writer for *The New Yorker*. Jane was much more interested in Mr. Johnson's connection with fascism during the Spanish Civil War than his architectural accomplishments. We conversed, and she agreed to a fair balance.

The next subject was photographer, Edward Steichen. Rupert's friend at the Museum of Modern Art had called to tell him that Mr. Steichen was enjoying an unusual period of clarity. In the 1960's, eighty-seven years was old, feeble, and without memory. We arranged a survey of the location and he invited us to lunch. We met him, his lovely wife, a former stewardess, who, years later, I would meet as a psychotherapist and a friend of Edward Albee.

Mr. Steichen wanted us to see Jergens pond, named for a

commercial assignment, and the little shad blow tree on the opposite side; he called it his "little girl", and photographed her growth during the seasons.

We experienced him as a gallant host, and scheduled the taping. As we left he said, "Of all the interviews I've had, you are the first to come talk with me."

Rupert Hitzig, Edward Steichen and Merrill during a break in filming of an interview with Steichen.

We brought the crew, and the interview went smoothly, filled with his memories. The report of Rupert's friend from MOMA was faultless. And, by this time, I was doing my own interviews.

I must add that, during this time of fevered activity, I had a personal life too. I had limited time and I spent it on performances: theater, dance and music and dinners with friends.

When I was still in Philadelphia, I would make infrequent trips to New York. On one of those trips a friend took me to see the *Fantasticks*, a simple Off-Broadway musical that had developed a wide following. The boy who played the lead was good-looking, his acting was in character and convincing, his singing was unaffected and winning. He was captivating and I was attracted; he released my sleeping romanticism. My friend introduced us; his name was Ty, named by his mother for Tyrone Power. I was effusive, probably too effusive and I think he thought of me as a "dirty old man" who lusted for him and he was not far off the mark.

When I moved to New York, I contacted him. We met, became acquainted and discovered that we had many of the same interests and passions. Soon we became boyfriends, my first. He was a talented actor and singer with possibilities for expanding each of those talents. I became his mentor. His career was rising and he played the youngest son in the first Broadway production of *The Lion in Winter*. From the beginning we were wise: he lived in his small apartment and I lived in my small apartment. After five years of intense interacting, the ardor slowly cooled and we went our own different directions. I think he wanted to be with someone closer to his own age. I continued to build my career, but I realized that I could not do what I planned to do if I were married with children, or even had a significant other of either gender.

CAMERA 3

The centerpiece of the WCBS programming was *Camera 3*, first broadcast in 1953, during the days when CBS solicited programs from their owned stations. When Los Angeles joined the network, all of its programming originated from the network. Somehow, *Camera 3* slipped through the cracks and continued. The choice of programming was the producer's in his "walk through the marketplace of ideas". The sequence of early, outstanding producers developed an exceptional and valuable series. When I arrived in 1962, I was not impressed with the program; it seemed tarnished and tired. Were producers using it as stepping-stone to a more successful commercial career? In those days ambitious directors thought soap operas could lead them to the golden land of movies. I didn't want to direct movies in Hollywood. I was told, "You must be crazy. Everybody wants to direct movies." I didn't; I wanted to direct first-rate television.

In 1967 the producership opened and I was asked several times to take the job. I was reluctant. I told The Suits (remember them from Philadelphia? They were the business bosses) that "The ship is listing and it needs to be put right." They offered once more and added, "Perhaps you don't think you can do it." **That did it**. I rushed into the arena with nose snorting fire and sword aloft.

Devising the programs was not the only problem: the program was broadcast fifty-two Sundays each year; the four Sundays in August were the only dates repeats could be scheduled. That meant forty-eight original programs a year. The budget for each program was $25,000, a pittance even then and not much more than the original 1953 budget. Careful financial planning was called for. In Philadelphia I allotted a portion of my budget for programs with new ideas, projects and people. Now, I was stingy each week—mostly by buying acquisitions so that I could splurge on something of substance. That's quite different from today's bottom-line thinking, which a colleague once said, "Came from the genius of the Harvard Business School, searching for ways to make more profit."

My early concern was about the audience; was anybody watching? I wanted to know about them: their work, their education, especially, their interests. I wanted to make programs for them. I took my curiosity to the CBS people who gathered such information. The reply was an exasperated, "For Crissakes, Merrill, go away. You have only two million viewers"

The pressure I felt was dissipated. I didn't have to make programs for ratings. I could explore and find informative themes, ideas and people. I was stimulated by the challenges and I was encouraged to take risks. Even if I had a flop one Sunday, I knew that I would be back the next Sunday with another favored thought.

When I began, I was sure that I didn't have enough ideas to get through the first season. A year later, I had four times the ideas needed. Many came from friendly suggestions, but I usually refused more than I accepted. Once I had decided the direction and tone for the series, ideas gushed.

The opportunities were in New York, which was rich with possibilities for adapting productions that existed. Original production was on a shoestring. The Suits recognized that I needed a playmate; so John Musilli was plucked from staff elsewhere and assigned to the show. I made half of the shows and he made half. We and our interests were exact opposites. John's were more literary; mine more performing arts. John was more passive; I was more aggressive. We talked, argued, laughed and learned to get along—and even like each other. That continued even after 1971 when I was appointed Executive Director.

Directing Ruby Dee for Camera 3

We tried to select from what was happening in music, dance, drama and literature, painting and sculpture. If asked, "Why are you doing so much music and not painting?" The answer was, "Music is where it's happening not painting."

Fortunately, The Suits didn't interfere with the selection of programs. My thought was, "I'm blessed. I'm on at 11AM Sunday morning when the television executives are on the golf course and the churchgoers are in their pews." Nobody complained, although one friendly executive said, "Hey, I saw your show Sunday. Do the boys upstairs know you're doing that kind of thing?" He was asking about the Sunday I programmed a Valle-Inclan's play in Spanish; the subtext was necrophilia.

My great good fortune was that, at that time, CBS had a contract orchestra and a resident conductor, Alfredo Antonini, who encouraged me to use it. I had heard Alicia de Larrocha, one of the piano giants of the day, play Mozart's final concerto with Boulez and the New York Philharmonic. It was glorious. Pierre Boulez (more of him later) encouraged me to invite her. But *Camera 3* had a problem. Although it may have been my embarrassment, no one who appeared on the program was paid more than $500, a favored nations policy. I invited Alicia and she accepted. That was when I had a thought that, perhaps, the great artists only incidentally do what they do for money. We taped Alicia's masterful performance. We laughed a lot and she called me Mister Broadway. Brockway, Broadway? She's Spanish, so it's possible.

Antonini was the conductor of the orchestra that appeared with Beverly Sills at Lewisohn Stadium in years past. Alfredo urged me to invite Miss Sills. I did and she said yes; but that came with her idea for the program. She said she would like to sing four arias that had contributed to the success of her career. The first was an aria from Handel's opera *Guilio Cesare*, the second from Douglas Moore's *Ballad of Baby Doe*; the third from a Mozart opera and my memory has not retained the identity of the fourth. The program had great variety and the performance of Beverly (by that time Miss Sills had become Beverly), Alfredo and the CBS Orchestra were breathtaking.

Faubion Bowers was a distinguished author and the biographer of the composer, Scriabin. Before that, during World War II, he was Major Bowers and General MacArthur's aide, which is confirmed by the famed photo of the general sloshing through the surf with Major Bowers on his right. The photo is called *MacArthur Returns*.

After the war Faubion remained in Japan, became friends with the leading Kabuki actors, met and married the daughter of the Indian ambassador to Japan (Santha Rama Rau, who became a famed writer) and explored the wonders of the East. In 1952 he published *Theater in the East*, which was the first introduction of eastern arts to the west.

Faubion came to see me with a program idea: a Chinese performing group that he would introduce and explicate the performance. I was intrigued: it was different, entertaining and seriously informative. We determined to continue our collaboration and that included: Japan's *Classical Bunraku Puppet Theater*, *The Ritual Athletes of Iran*, *Dancers of Bali*— among many others. My favorite was *The Dark Chopin*, which Faubion wrote and narrated and Garrick Ohlsen played. By this time Faubion and I were lifelong friends.

A decade later Faubion's friends, the growing-older Kabuki stars, agreed to filming them in an historic Kabuki play. We raised the money from the National Endowment for the Humanities. My assistant, Glenn Berenbeim, went along to lend his considerable skills to the filming of *Terakoya*. The experience was unsettling: Faubion spoke fluent Japanese; Glenn and I didn't. Our translator was a young man whose first language was German; apparently his Japanese was satisfactory, for I had no trouble communicating with the three cameramen. They were remarkably professional. I had record tapes of what we were recording which I could stop and show the tasks for each and the framings. Each had paper and a pen. Each held the pen touching his face until he began to write. I learned that the pen would stay near the face until he understood what I wanted. Once understood and noted, it was never forgotten. Note: the Japanese frame the picture wider, much wider than Americans. They were surprised by my tighter framings; they called it "American framing".

The adventure was an informative and rewarding visit to Japan and the Japanese people. Faubion was a superb guide and I was thrilled to be working in the Kabukiza, the performance space of Kabuki.

PIERRE BOULEZ

I first learned about Pierre Boulez when I was a student at Columbia; that he was a remarkably talented *avant-garde* composer and an *enfant terrible* in Paris. My favorite tale occurred after a concert of Pierre's music: Pierre hurled himself over a line of chairs to meet the source of loud, negative comments: a woman with a large flowery hat. "It's a very pretty hat, too bad it's on such a stupid head." Years later I was in London where I saw the notice for his English debut as a conductor; which I thought unthinkable, especially since his whole program was all Beethoven. The next day's reviews were loudly approving, "unqualifiedly brilliant!"

In the 1970s when I was at *Camera 3*, I went to Hunter College to hear Boulez conduct *Concerto for Nine Instruments* by Webern. Afterwards, I introduced myself and asked him if he would have an interest in recording it for television. He said he believed in the power of television for contemporary music "If you present it, they'll believe it;" but that he would rather record Schoenberg's *Pierrot*

Lunaire, "One of the great masterpieces of the 20th century and nobody knows it." My job was to find the mezzo-soprano. That resulted in Jan de Gaetani who sang for Boulez and he invited her to join the project.

Pierrot Lunaire was a short piece. I needed a filler to round it out to half an hour. The musicians were the CBS orchestra and they were meeting Pierre for the first time. I suggested I make a short documentary about the first rehearsal, the first time the conductor and the musicians meet each other, because "It's actual; it's real." We did it; I edited it and it was boring. Later Martha Graham would tell me "Art is Artifice." Soon after, Pierre was appointed Music Director of the New York Philharmonic. His corporate task was to sell tickets. His personal task was to sell contemporary music.

I heard a Philharmonic concert after he had been appointed. He programmed Berg's *Lyric Suite*, Mozart's last piano concerto with Alicia de Larroccha and a long piece by Varese, that "autocratic, shaggy-haired, self-proclaimed messiah of modernism". Clearly, the audience had come to hear the Mozart. The program order was Berg, Mozart, Intermission, then Varese. At the intermission the audience streamed out. Afterwards, I spoke with Pierre. He knew they had left before the Varese, but he smilingly said, "They had to listen to the Berg."

Pierre liked to program opposites. The next year his choice for *Camera 3* was Haydn and Stravinsky. I needed only five minutes of filler. Before I could suggest anything, he said, "Let me do it." After his rehearsal, after all the musicians were comfortable with the music, Pierre remembered that a rehearsal documentary was needed. The musicians chortled and asked if they should pretend they were sight-reading. Pierre assured them that they should play to the extent of their abilities. Then, he did something astonishingly brilliant. He rehearsed only the transitions between sections, the most vulnerable parts of a performance. That's usually where the change of tempo occurs. The musicians were challenged and played with spontaneity. Any attentive listener would hear the essence of the often-misunderstood classical sonata principle, in a five-minute essay. So you see, real is not always best, as Martha often said. Pierre asked me to accompany him to the premiere of a new piece he wrote for the Chamber Music Society of Lincoln Center. He had limited rehearsal time; so he had invested it in the difficult sections. He had yet to hear the piece from beginning to end, but it didn't seem to bother him. He trusted himself and he trusted the musicians. The performance went swimmingly.

Merrill with Pierre Boulez

Pierre was the purest man I've ever known. Joan Peyser, a graduate classmate of mine wanted to write his biography; she asked him and he agreed. He also introduced her to his family and close friends. Later, she came to me, furious; she could find no dirt. I think she was sure she would find that he was homosexual. I told her, "He's a monk." She stalked off to write her next biography about Leonard Bernstein.

I remember Pierre for his respect: for his musicians and for the music he conducted. At that time Bernstein was near the height of his Mahler hysteria. Pierre always referred to the composer as "the great Father, Mahler." It sounded disparaging. Later I noted that Pierre began to conduct Mahler. I suspect that he studied the scores and found what he could respect; for his interpretations are simpler, the sound is less mushy (I can hear the inner parts) and, for me, more deeply felt. In a recent (March 2009) *New York Times* review, Anthony Tomasini wrote about the insightful performances of the very scores he once disdained, saying, "When Mr. Boulez conducts, typically he is seized with a desire to show exactly what it is in the piece he has chosen that intrigues him as a composer. (Or provokes him, as the case may be.)"

In May 2009 the *New York Times* quoted Pierre's statement about Mahler, "In the noble world of the symphony, he sowed the bad seeds of theatricality, sentimentality, vulgarity, insolent and unbearable disorder." *The Times'* critic added: "And, he meant it as a compliment." In 1973 Pierre said essentially the same things to me and he didn't mean it as a compliment.

Our collaborations continued until the end of his tenure with the Philharmonic. He was extraordinarily generous in sharing his knowledge with me. He and, later, Balanchine were superior teachers. Each took me to a higher level of understanding. To answer my question, Pierre once explained that his music notation was unusually small because "It doesn't waste energy." That was the same with his conducting. He doesn't wave his arms theatrically. He trusts his players and gives them instructions with small, precise motions. He leaves the theatricality to the music.

One day we were talking about Stravinsky's *Rite of Spring*, an extremely difficult score. Almost every measure (bar) is in a different meter: for example, 3/4, 6/8, 5/16, etc. Sometimes conductors rebar for their own personal reasons, usually to simplify. I asked Pierre, "Do you rebar?" His speedy answer, "I do <u>not</u> rebar. Bernstein rebars."

Camera 3 continued scheduling what we believed was important and good for the program. When I planned the Valle-Inclan play in Spanish with the hint of necrophilia, there was a lot of negotiation with the censor about that one. Censorship was called "Program Practices", and there was a lot of it around. Many directors started by snorting fire. That would come to no good. My strategy was: Bring them in early, don't try to fool or bully them and negotiate. I explained and smiled a lot. I found that most censors were willing to help you get what you wanted. Some of the rules, especially for Sunday morning, were strong then. When I bumped my head on one of them, I had to change.

In the early 1970s I began a *Camera 3* intermittent series called *Aspects of the New Consciousness*, periodic programs based on observations of how our minds were being stretched by the arts and sciences. John Cage spoke about "New Music", Alvin Toffler about "Future Shock" and genetic engineering was another subject. One program presented Humphrey Osmond, a pioneer in the study of schizophrenia and his work with hallucinogens. Humphrey had introduced Aldous Huxley to mescaline; which became a book, *The Doors of Perception*. I spoke to Humphrey; I told him I'd observed young people who had taken LSD (acid) and I was stirred by accounts of their sharpening self-observation. I told him I was flirting with the idea but felt I was too old, that I had too much in my memory bank and did not know how to go about it. He encouraged me to explore, but advised me against using street acid: "too much adulteration." He suggested I call Dr. Ross McLain, the director of a private hospital outside of Vancouver, Canada. Note: By this date, use of hallucinogens in America was illegal, except for terminal cancer and one other, army-related reason. The work of Timothy Leary at Harvard was a compelling reason for the ban.

I called Doctor McLain; he asked me a few pointed questions (essentially to find out if I were schizophrenic and would not be considered for treatment) and invited me to "Come out, but give us a few days warning." I arrived at the hospital eager to begin. The first three days were filled with physical and psychological tests; I knew I was in good hands. I asked the doctor, "What is a bad trip?" (Trip and tripping were buzzwords in those days). His answer was, "A bad trip is what you came here <u>not</u> to have." He explained further that a bad trip is receiving more information from yourself than you can process and then you do destructive things, usually to yourself, such as jumping out of a window or off a roof.

D-Day arrived: After drinking a cup of tea with an additive which was understood to be acid that would send me on a trip, I was made comfortable, lying down, with a cover because body heat is carefully monitored during the trip. The experience began. (I neglected to mention that my eyes were blindfolded and the trip was being guided by music from earphones). The first part of the trip was my body's defenses against the invader. It was a brave and rousing fight, but the invader won out. My image was that I was urinating the Hoover Dam to overflowing. From that point the wet clothes were left behind.

We settled down to thirteen hours of hallucination: I was floating down a river, exploring myself in pictures fearful and anxious, laughing and silly, hopeful and pessimistic, arrogant and unconfident—it was all there. The music guided the exploration.

By the end I was exhausted. The coming-down music was uplifting works by Mahler and the attendant showed me a real rose and it was weeping—or that's how I interpreted the breathing drops of moisture. I was also flooded with feelings that I had guarded and kept secret: my father was the one human being I loved the most.

When I could talk, I didn't have to. The doctor knew I was shaky and bewildered. He arranged a car, a sleeping bag and a box of food. He told me to drive to Vancouver Island and find a camping place on the beach. "Talk to no one, read nothing, listen to nothing and come back when you want to talk."

As I lay alone on the beach, looking up at the clouds during the day and the clouds and stars at night, a slow, mysterious alteration began to take place in me. What I was feeling was best written by Carl Sandburg in his introduction to *The Family of Man:*

"I am! I have come through! I belong! I am a member of the family."

That's the way I feel now when I look at the clouds and stars in Santa Fe.

I wanted *Camera 3* to be on the cutting edge. For example, I believed that the Open Theater was one of the important theater developments of that time. Joe Chaikin, the leader, came from the earlier Living Theater, the celebrated experimental company. I told him how important I thought his group's work was and that I wanted to record as much of it as possible. He listened; then I learned that the company had had an unpleasant television experience with PBS. After pondering it, he agreed.

Our first project was *Terminal*, a study of death. This upset a number of viewers, understandably. Joe and I liked to work together so we recorded other pieces until the group disbanded.

Joe taught me something important. One day during rehearsal he said, "You look troubled." I told him I was; I didn't know how to place cameras for a particular sequence that started at A and ended at G. Joe said, "Don't worry about it. A to C and G are traffic; the actors are just getting in and out of position. The images you care about are D, E and F."

The company worked in images and its members were teachers who helped me separate the important from the unimportant and act on it. Then, I was dealing with a stage presentation; now, with tape and editing, I wouldn't even shoot A to C and G. Today the *Camera 3* library is the only place the work of the Open Theater can be found.

I made several programs in difficult circumstances and trying conditions, a wonderful way to broaden my skills as a director. Working with certain people challenged me. Boulez was one. I was stretched by George Crumb's song cycle for voice and instruments, *Ancient Voices of Children*. The challenge was to make what was essentially a radio show visually compelling. The singer was Jan De Gaetani, whom I had worked with when she sang *Pierrot Lunaire* with Boulez. I admired her work then and, especially, now, having heard her recording of *Ancient Voices of Children*, which George Crumb had written for her.

At that time the video synthesizer was a fad (it could be programmed to make abstract video pictures) and I thought it might be used appropriately for two instrumental sections. I knew Ron Hays who was an operating exponent and he agreed to work with me. I wanted the colors and shapes related to the structural elements of the music. I didn't want a non-musician's rampant impressionism. The result was basic introduction to the synthesizer. The program was unusual and distinctive. Jan paid me a compliment that I still remember. "You are a true friend of music." I would like to have developed more sophistication, but the synthesizer went out of fashion as fast as it came in.

DANCE

I was bitten by the dance bug during my undergraduate years at Columbia. Martha Graham was my first experience with concert dance. At *Camera 3*, I wanted to do more dance, but it was difficult and expensive. All television studios have cement floors and dancers can't dance on cement without flirting with injury. They also can't dance as many hours as an instrumentalist can play or an actor can act.

I had a dance floor built. It was rudimentary, but it got the dancers off the cement. The schedule was hard for them; we never had more than one day to record half an hour. Later, at *Dance in America* we had a more ample schedule and we were pleased if we recorded twelve minutes a day.

Twyla Tharp and I made a program, but I didn't have enough experience and technique to handle her free-swinging choreography. I was embarrassed and disappointed. I later said that, "I buried that tape so deep that even a hog snorting for truffles will not be able to find it."

Twyla and I would work together two more times, for *Dance in America* and for CBS CABLE, but the first time set the pattern: we would end the project angry with each other and not speak for at least a year and then there would be an unexpected meeting and she would say, "What were we angry about and are we still?" That was my cue to say, "I don't remember and I'm not."

Twyla Tharp during filming

MAURICE BEJART

My experiences with Maurice Bejart began unexpectedly when I received a phone call from his management in Brussels. They asked if I would consider a project with Maurice—at their expense. I didn't know much about the Ballet of the 20th Century except that it was popular in Europe. The offer was generous; so I said I would like to consider it. This was followed by an invitation—at their expense—to go to Brussels to see the company and meet Maurice. I saw no ethical problem with my all-expenses-paid trip; so I accepted.

I found the company, which usually performs in the round, to be one of winning professionals, the ballets to be theatrical and entertaining and Maurice to be charming. We connected immediately. Soon I heard the reason for the call: Clive Barnes, a London dance critic, who had emigrated to the *New York Times*, where he was the big Pooh-Bah, didn't like Maurice's work and said so in print. Simple. Maurice's management wanted him to become familiar in America. I was not a fan of Mr. Barnes' criticism, but that was not a factor; I felt that Maurice's work was superior to much of the European dance that was exported to America. Arlene Croce of *The New Yorker* called it "Euro trash," and I further felt that America should have the opportunity to make up its own mind about the work and the company.

Maurice and I conferred and agreed upon the dances to be filmed. I became familiar with the recording space (in the round) and the editing studio where I would be putting it together. Coincidentally and happily, Dyane Gray, a principal dancer in the company, had been a student at the Philadelphia Dance Academy and the choreographer of the first dance I directed for television. Also, Suzanne Farrell was there after leaving the New York City Ballet. It was a spirited reunion with both.

I returned: the program was filmed and edited with no unpleasant surprises. The program was broadcast and I have no memory of the response, but I do remember that I saw the company in New York and Maurice was dancing a carefree and devilish devil. The response was the usual: the critics hated it; the audience loved it. I have no clue whether the appearance on *Camera 3* speeded his appearance in America or not.

I returned to Brussels a few years later to film Maurice's new work, entitled *Nijinsky*. Again, the filming was in the round for several performances. This time Suzanne was the female lead. The surprise came in editing: in one performance she wore a white leotard; in another performance she wore black. Decades later—only recently—I asked her about it. She told me the white was a rehearsal, the black was a performance—or was it the other way around? Whatever? Mystery solved, but it was quite an editing quandary.

MERCE CUNNINGHAM

Merce Cunningham sent two emissaries together before he appeared to propose a project which intrigued me: to divide the television screen into four equal sections, two above two below, each with different information about the dance. The process was intensely engrossing. The result was uncertain. How many sections would a viewer absorb? My number was three.

Later in life, when I would enthuse about dance, a listening friend would say, "There are two kinds of people; those who like to see bodies move and those who don't give a damn."

Around 1973-74 we began hearing rumblings of doom. A Suit at CBS News began to ask, informally, "Why do they have this time slot? Who do they report to?" We were sure that our hiding place in the cracks was about to be discovered. Other troubling signs appeared: periodically the local station in Los Angeles would move us to 6AM Sunday morning. We had a loyal group of local viewers who bombarded the station with hate mail until we were restored to 11AM. Another unwelcome situation was in Boston where the local station pre-empted us every third week. We had begun two-, three- and in one case, four-part miniseries over successive Sundays. When a Boston viewer tuned in and found an episode pre-empted, he got pretty irate and didn't tune in anymore, but Boston was not Los Angeles. The time period was never restored. I knew the end was near.

Prelude to *Dance in America*

During the Christmas season of 1974, Jac Venza asked to see me. Jac was a former scenic designer at CBS and we had worked together there. In 1974 he was the Executive Producer of *Great Performances* at PBS/ WNET. He told me, "There's going to be a dance series initiated by the National Endowment for the Arts. It will most likely originate in New York." He then asked me to take a position on the series. Emile Ardolino had already worked for a year in writing the proposal. It was an extraordinary document, written to cover all bases, satisfy all requirements; yet somehow allow the producers freedom of choice. I hadn't known Emile before. He had some training in ballet, but his real skill was editing. I, of course, knew nothing about ballet; I didn't even like it very much. I always said, "Martha is mother's milk to me." I politely left out, "and, I don't drink anything else."

Joining WNET presented what could have been a charged situation. In order to get me to leave CBS after twenty-two years (where I had gotten my twenty-year Tiffany clock), Jac had to offer me the top job of the series. I'm sure he would have preferred that the top job would be a "co"- job. There was a hint of that until I said, "I don't co- anything." Jack left Emile and me alone after saying, "Figure out your titles." We agreed that I would be Series Producer and Emile would be Coordinating Producer.

The plan was that we would be responsible for four programs a year (the first year, there were five) for two years, the length of the grant. I would produce and direct one unit with an associate producer and Emile would produce the other unit with a director to be chosen for each project. I asked and Jac agreed that Judy Kinberg could come with me from CBS to be my associate producer. Judy had been with me for years since she graduated from Hunter College. She had started as the *Camera 3* secretary then advanced to production assistant.

The list of possible directors was short and most of their experience had been with television specials. Jerry Schnur had directed American Ballet Theatre's *Closeup in Time*, the year before. I believe he also directed an Alvin Ailey program before that. Gar Compton had some experience directing dance. Both of them were eager to join us. The series also planned to flush out other candidates.

When I told my mother I was planning to leave CBS without severance pay after twenty-two years, she was concerned; especially when I told her it was for only two years. She asked if I then planned to go back to CBS. When I told her no, she asked what I planned to do. I said, "Get another job." "My dear," she replied, "you are not a recent college graduate." I was fifty-two at the time. I had been in and out of psychotherapy since my Columbia days and the end of the war. Fortunately, I had a very good therapist who helped me get through this difficult period without separation anxiety. Later, he told me, "To leave CBS was the single most important decision of your life. By making that decision you will make subsequent difficult decisions much easier." This has proved to be true.

At CBS I was working for a program director who was a fan of my work, Bob Shay. He asked me if I was sure I wanted to leave. I told him I didn't know and he said, "I want to put you on consultancy for six months. If you change your mind, if it's not what you thought it would be, then come back." I thought that was a most generous offer. There are so many stories of corporate bloodletting; I was fortunate to have such a different experience. I went to WNET in June, 1975. By January 1976 I could say, "I want to stay" and Shay appointed Roger Englander to replace me on *Camera 3.*

Dance in America: First Year

*D*ance in America (DIA) was funded by the National Endowment for the Arts (NEA), the Corporation for Public Broadcasting (CPB) and EXXON. In return for their money:

> NEA wanted QUALITY
> CPB wanted QUANTITY
> EXXON wanted TUTUS

Jac Venza was, by office, the peacemaker and Emile and I decided what would be best for the series. First, we discussed the performance priorities. We decided our first priority would be the dancers and their care; our second would be what they would dance—the choreography and our third would be where they would be dancing—the production setting.

Our first broadcast was to be in January 1976 with the Joffrey Ballet. We believed it had the most mainstream appeal. The first one scheduled to tape was Martha Graham in October 1975. It was a coup to get her and to get her first, but it was not easy. Martha opened our first meeting with, "I don't collaborate." Apparently she had heard the announcement of our plan to collaborate with the choreographers. Martha made it clear that we had to play by her rules or there was no game. First, she wanted a longer program than any other company, ninety minutes, not an hour. Next, she didn't want to do medleys; she wanted to present only complete works. When Emile mumbled that we were Public Broadcasting and didn't have the networks' resources, she replied, "We must entertain the thought that you don't have enough money to do this project." We hung in there and negotiated an agreement and an October taping date.

Almost immediately a representative from her company called and announced that Martha would like to postpone; apparently, an engagement for the company had come up. Emile was shaken: "Merrill, don't let her do this." I asked why he was so bothered. "She's over eighty years old," he said. His implication was clear, but obviously he was not a Martha watcher. I told him that Martha didn't have death on her calendar. "Don't sweat it; if she goes away between now and then, I'll give her the God-damndest, biggest memorial anyone's ever seen."

After Martha postponed, we scheduled Twyla Tharp, which was part of the master plan. I had big-mouthed that, if we were able to make thirteen programs, we could cover the major ground of concert dance: three major ballet companies, the two best regional companies, the four best modern dance companies and a dance history documentary. These all were categories the proposal had promised. We had planned that some of our shows would be shared by two companies: Twyla and Eliot Feld, for example. They both thought sharing was a wonderful idea, but not with each other. We ended with a separate program with Twyla, combined with a documentary about jazz dance. Arlene Croce, *New Yorker* dance critic, agreed to write the narration. She was a big Twyla fan

Twyla in rehearsal

A bigger drama than any of us were aware of was developing: few television studios in New York could handle productions of our size. In fact, the only satisfactory one was NBC, Brooklyn, which was housing soap operas. None of us believed that we could uproot them for concert dance on PBS. Coincidentally, *The Adams Chronicles* was just finishing shooting at a film studio on Tenth Avenue and Fifty-Fourth Street. It was a big film sound stage. Jac Venza, who was also the executive producer of the *Chronicles*, persuaded us to look it over. The space was perfect and our new floor fit in beautifully.

The floor was another drama that we thought had been resolved. "Dancers don't dance on cement" was old news. But what do they dance on? We asked each major company to send us their crabbiest, most complaining dancer. We held tests and found that pointe shoe dancers want different things from barefoot dancers. We negotiated a compromise, a floor that every method of dancer could live with. It was essentially a three-tiered sandwich of plywood, foam rubber and plywood, topped by linoleum. But that was not the end of the drama. The floor had to be designed and painted. Traditionally, a dance stage floor is battleship gray strips of linoleum often joined by non-matching strips of gaffers' tape. Ugly! Television exposes and aggravates the ugliness. In order to paint the linoleum and have it sealed and permanent, the facedown side of the linoleum became the face-up side. That was good enough for barefoot dancers, but when a ballerina sticks her wooden toe into the floor, she exposes a tar base that will forever record her tracks. It was a mess that took years to sort out.

Back to Tenth Avenue and Fifty-Fourth Street: the floor was down, the beautiful new unblemished cyclorama was in place. I looked and cried with happiness. I went home and slept beautifully that night. Next morning we began. Remember, this was the first day of shooting for the series that was going to take dancers and their fans to the moon.

Twyla and I agreed that we would tape each rehearsal and show it to the dancers, so that each one could see, rather than be told, what he or she had done. That took more time, but it was a more intelligent and humane way of including dancers in the correction process. I also wanted the cameramen to see how each one's work fit into the whole. We were an ensemble and playing chamber music. Videotape was the answer to that.

Within two hours I had annoyance. The top of the cyclorama was lighted, the bottom was lighted, but the middle wasn't. The dancers, the cameras, Twyla and I continued to rehearse. The time came when we had to record something or go sour—"Not possible! Lighting needs more time." The annoyance became trouble and at the end of the day we suspended "until technical difficulties can be worked out." The house could not handle the demands of the great lighting designer Jennie Tipton's plot.

*Twyla and Merrill
in rehearsal*

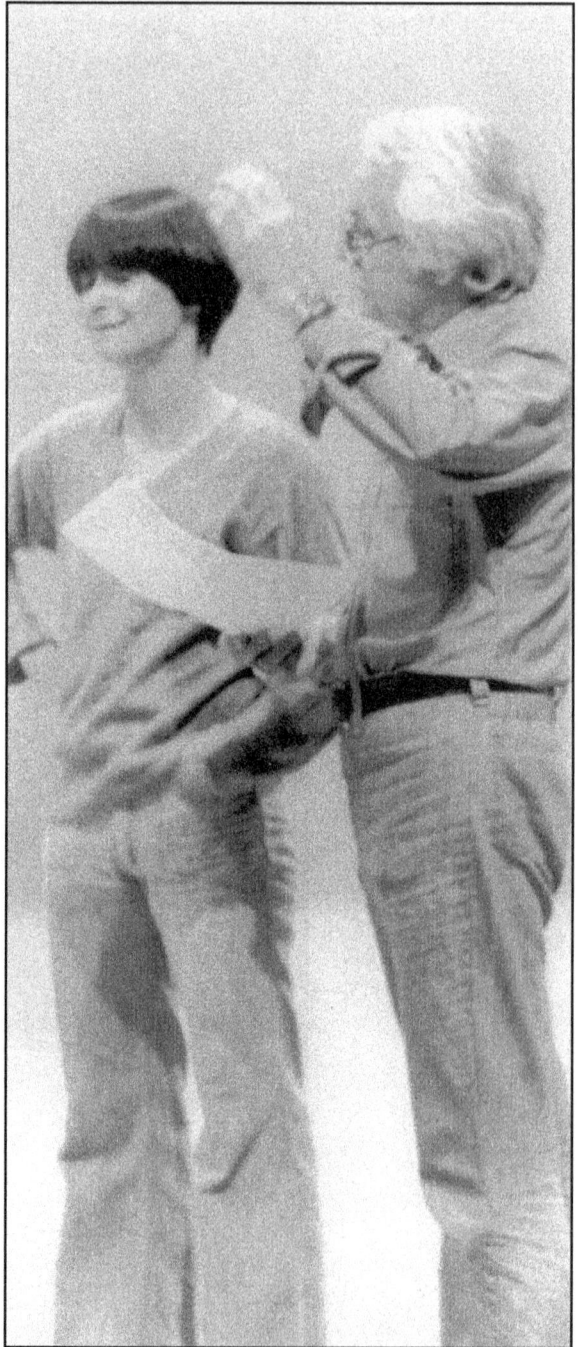

Twyla and Merrill
in rehearsal

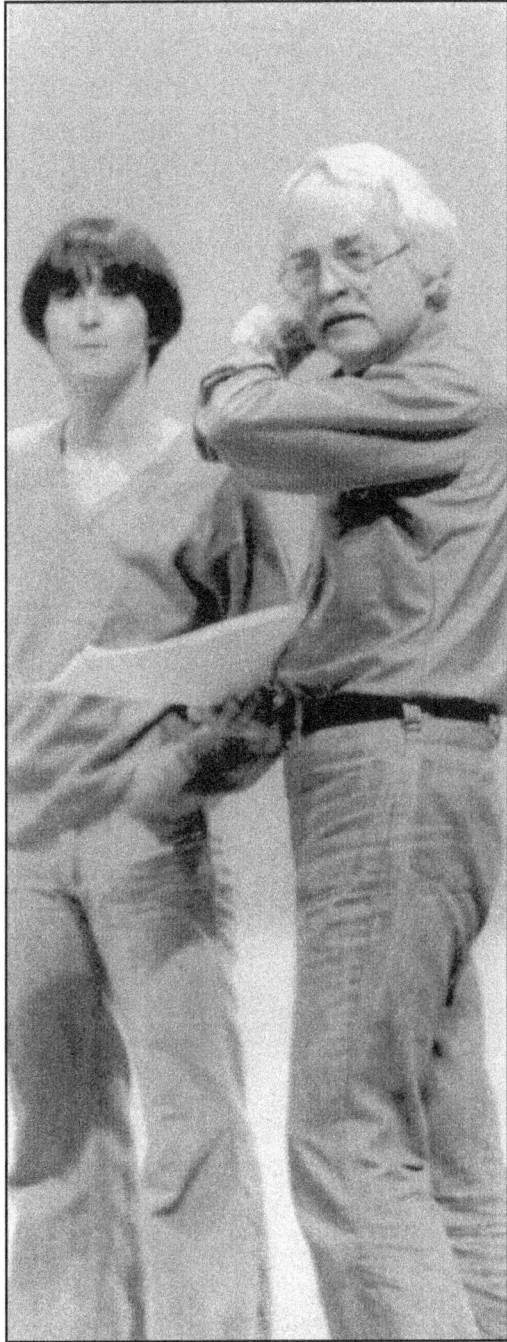

*Twyla and Merrill
in rehearsal*

A few years later the theater manager told me, "You were dead from the time you came in" I had unprintable thoughts about JacVenza, who brought all participants and me into this doomed situation.

This was dancing; the lighting was different from drama. This was not easy to explain to the irate Twyla with her lawyer on one side and her company manager on the other. We reconvened after two days (at $30,000 a day. I was behind before I started) of feverish work with lighting equipment and we limped through, but the result was only marginally satisfactory.

I switched the cameras live, because that was the way I had always done it. When I viewed the tapes later, I decided once again that real is not always best; isolated cameras—one camera to one tape machine instead of three cameras recording on one tape machine—was available to me, but I'd never done that and I didn't take advantage of the opportunity. I had always thought "live event", now I began to think "created event from live elements". I began to suspect that the technology could be my friend and the magic of editing could liberate me.

Bob Joffrey's company was scheduled to record after Twyla. Bob had heard of our struggle, stopped by, watched and said, "I'm not going into that studio." We later learned that before *The Adams Chronicles*, *The Exorcist* had been filmed there.

Our backup space was in Austin, Texas. I was scheduled to direct with Emile producing, but I was a psychological wreck. Emile, good friend and producer, came to me and pointed out, "You are in no condition to do this show." I knew he was right. We asked Jerry Schnur. He, Emile, JacVenza, the crew and dancers went to Texas for another horrendous experience: big space but inexperienced crew, inadequate service facilities for the dancers and unacceptable technical facilities, including a crane from Hollywood in the 30s (it took four men to operate it). Now, Jerry loved a crane; he loved to see it move. We joked about his planning fifteen camera positions in a single crane move. It's one thing if the subject is standing still; quite another to coordinate those fifteen positions with dancers who are moving. Fold in Jerry's perfectionism and the difficulty of getting anything on tape is understandable. Anyway, they all straggled back from Texas. Jac, Emile and the accounting department were all wrecks, but Jerry's perfectionism was intact. The show was finished because of the masterly editing of Girish Bhargava. From that time on I referred to Girish as "our secret weapon". Jerry Schnur never directed another *Dance in America* production.

The Joffrey Ballet became the first *Dance in America* program. It proved to be so successful that Bob suggested a study, which the NEA sponsored. The study discovered that many people who had never seen The Joffrey Ballet, saw them on television and decided they wanted to see them in person. They also preferred to see them dance the ballets they'd seen on television.

On watching the telecast, I was not comfortable with our decision to present a mixed bag, a collection of small pieces. Merce Cunningham once advised me, "Never underestimate the intelligence of your audience. They're smarter than you think." Later we would find that our audience could indeed handle complete dances, some not so easy. At this time the prevailing thought was that the audience would turn us off if they didn't get a cherry in each chocolate. I must confess that I was a wimp, after all, *Camera 3* audiences averaged only two million people. I believed that in order to upgrade audience numbers you had to downgrade the material. Second, Jerry and I had very different directing styles because we looked at dancing with different eyes. Never ask one barber about another barber's haircut.

From our first two recording experiences we learned that we needed to make some changes. The idea of two units alternating was discarded: Emile produced, I directed, Judy Kinberg associate produced. Later, when Emile began to direct, he and I alternated as producer. This was for *DIA* money reasons: the more you do, the more you learn, the faster you become and the more money you save. I also threw out any plans I had to switch live after I witnessed Girish's skills. I adopted a new attitude toward the crane. Since the quality of the performance was our first priority, I determined: When the dancers are moving, the crane doesn't; when the dancers are relatively still, the crane can move. I never wanted a situation that the performers were intimidated by repeating a flawed crane move. This was part of our growing awareness of dancer energy. Dancers can't dance on and on; they tire—some more than others.

We began to record videotape during rehearsals. After the piece had been set in collaboration with the choreographer, we recorded it. That is what the director used to learn the piece; that is what he showed the cameramen when he gave them their shot sheets and showed them their tasks. This record tape saved a lot of wear and tear on the dancers.

Each of the choreographers wanted total artistic control. That, of course, we could not give them; since we were responsible for the money. Emile's proposal implied that the choreographers would have participation and that, we wanted. We wanted to follow the intentions of the choreographer, who we asked to collaborate with us. Decisions were arrived at by mutual agreement. It certainly was contractually loose, but we never had a serious incident because of it. Balanchine later told me about his horrendous experience in Germany where "The directors took my ballets and made their own film pieces. Why don't they choreograph their own ballets? Why are they taking my ballets?"

I had evolved the collaborative approach on *Camera 3*. I always included "In collaboration with" in the credits with Merce, with Twyla. I brought that with me to *DIA*, my years as an accompanist as my guide.

In the past, choreographers had been skeptical about television, about its intentions. This time they knew there was money and viewers for them. Their companies needed money and recognition. They also knew that *DIA* was nothing without them; we didn't have the dances. It was common sense that we work together. In the early days of television, on shows that presented dance, such as *The Bell Telephone Hour*, the choreographer didn't go to the studio with the dancers. The television director damned well did what he wanted. We originated the idea of the choreographer's participation as collaborator. I, for one, was delighted. My phrase was, "It is time to freshen the water." The water had gotten very stagnant, missing quality.

The choreographer was never a part of planning the shots. For me that was the director's prerogative and I resisted anything that hinted at rule by committee. With the exception of Twyla and Merce, none of the other choreographers had experience in plotting cameras; although, later, Balanchine told amusingly about his Goldwyn days in Hollywood. Twyla's experience had been with a single camera. She didn't understand the workings of multi-camera shoots. Merce did; he had precise ideas and most of them were usable. Three-camera rotation can be a tricky thing. Peter Martins got the idea and he was rewarding to work with. The others didn't want to get involved; they just wanted to be sure their piece was being well served.

I had long been aware that differences of opinion and arguments in the studio could eat a lot of precious time. There are a number of people hanging out in the studio with a pipeline to the producer and each one has an opinion. I've had shouting matches with producers who thought shots should be different and in a different order than I was showing them. This time I determined that, because each camera was being recorded individually, everyone could see the materials being recorded, but the edited version at that moment existed only in my head. If the producer saw something that I was not shooting and pointed it out, I would arrange to shoot it. That didn't mean I would use it in the final edit, but it saved a helluva lot of arguing time in the studio.

It was also in recording Martha that the rudiments of a system for televising dance emerged. The last program of the year was the Pennsylvania Ballet. It was generally ignored. We were relieved because it teetered on boring.

The key to solving the difficulties of recording an hour or ninety minute program, with diminishing concentration and energy, is feeding, resting and retraining the dancers, as any difficulty came from their training of bringing themselves emotionally and physically up for an evening performance. The television studio was quite another routine: after an early class, makeup and wardrobe, we began to rehearse, then tape at 11AM. We usually worked in five-minute dance sections: rehearse, then tape. That meant the dancers relax for rehearsal, are up for performance and so on. That's very wearing, both physically and emotionally. Musicians can do it, but they sit and doodle. Actors should be able to do it, but some of the doing is questionable. But dancers really do it. Emile, Judy and I loved the dancers and respected their work; Judy was the housemother who looked after getting them to and from the studio, their food breaks and their rest periods. We wanted them to be happy.

At *DIA* I learned flexibility. There is no "one way", but don't try to tell that to a young director just starting out. I began to suspect that directing is a lot about editing, not only tape and film, but ideas. A long-ago friend of mine, John Stix, had brilliant successes in his mid-thirties directing Helen Hayes. During a rehearsal Miss Hayes stopped and said, "John, stop directing me. Just edit me." I think that's typical of young directors—they only want to direct. My definition of a good director is one smart enough or lucky enough to get great material and a great cast and know how to edit.

Martha Graham and Twyla Tharp (who studied with Martha for about twenty minutes) were two suns in different galaxies. At our first meeting Martha, who announced, "I don't collaborate." turned out to be a superb collaborator. We placed three monitors side by side on the studio floor so that she could see what each camera was recording. She didn't want to be in the control room, as she knew that Ron Protas would harass me. Ron was her protector who refused, later, to hire me to make Martha's biography, for reasons I never understood. She didn't know the editing plan in my mind and she didn't seem to care. She wanted to see that all was going well. She was checking the dancers and the quality of their performance. Martha was helpful to me because she was so verbal. We had agreed on a program. I had an easy time with *Appalachian Spring* but a tough time trying to figure out *Diversion of Angels*. What is the subtext? I went to Martha and said, "Tell me everything you can about *Diversion of Angels*." She talked and remembered, talked and philosophized. Talked. It was a story, a drama of the three forces of a woman. Then I understood how to shoot it. Martha's was the first program we taped in Nashville. After two disastrous experiences elsewhere, we found a home at the new Grand Ole Opry. There were two large performance spaces, both designed with awareness of future needs. The studio was a jewel with a ceiling high enough to accommodate an ample cyclorama. Dancing needs, yea demands, height behind the dancers. Then the auditorium stage was even larger and could hold more dancers and more production support. Little did we think we would find Heaven on the outskirts of Nashville.

This was the first time we began to record in a different way. The practice had been to rehearse and tape movements. Then we discovered that it was more efficient to break a movement into organic sections, rarely more than five minutes each. The length would depend on the difficulty for the dancers and cameras and the congeniality with the music.

Choreographers, at first, thought this would disrupt the flow of the dancing, but they soon came to see that, by isolating a risky section, they could create their own perfect performance. They wouldn't have to settle for a second rate performance sandwiched between two first-rate sections. Even Mikhail Baryshnikov asked to have an especially treacherous section isolated (that was later in Balanchine's *Prodigal Son*).

Martha liked the control it gave her over the performance. *Frontier* was a signature piece; she later said it was the most personal piece to her. During the rehearsal she became upset by the performance. She was dismayed that today's dancers don't dig into the ground; they're "so balletically trained. She's floating away." *Frontier* is a real dig-into-the-ground piece. We dismissed everyone but the cameramen and Martha and I went to the control room by ourselves. There, with a talkback to the floor, she could guide the performance in the same way the control tower guides a plane's landing. It was glorious to watch her do it. When she saw the results, she said, "I didn't even notice your edits." Both Girish and I were overjoyed, "Martha, that is the highest compliment you could ever pay us." That's what we tried to do: make the edits organic and not call attention to us.

I preferred not to have the choreographer around till we had a rough cut. I had a plan and I wanted a chance to show it before anybody picked at it. I think of myself as an interpreter. I don't think there is such a thing as objectivity. Each person sees from his or her own center. And I don't think that is something that requires an apology. I knew that, with each dance, I was making a video interpretation. I tried to do what I had learned as an accompanist: get in sync with the singer. I tried to get in sync with the choreographer's intentions. I avoided anything tricky that would take attention away from the piece. In accompanying circles, if someone compliments your accompaniments, you are probably playing too loud— balance your sound with the performer's. There was an incident with Balanchine during the taping of *Divertimento No.15* in the third season. The choreography was "turn, turn". One virtuoso did "turn, turn, turn". Balanchine said, "No, dear, two only; third time is a trick."

Looking back on the first season, I had no idea whether we were getting anywhere. I was operating on my experience with dance, which had been limited. I was learning from mistakes and mishaps, but doing led to new ideas. It was process at work.

I was disappointed with the Joffrey show and I was disappointed with the Twyla show. The jazz documentary of the Twyla show was brilliant but overpowered the live dancing. Martha was the third program and I liked it. We were beginning to get some place. The critical response was enthusiastic. I think that was the first time that "prestigious series" appeared in print. Martha set the respectability level.

Onward and Upward

One day Emile came to me and said, "I'd like to direct." I was delighted. As the sole director I was feeling the pressure. He continued, "I have worked with Jerry and Gar and I know their approaches, but I would like to use your system." My "system" was a detailed procedure I had developed for preparing and recording concert dance (see attachments). I was doubly delighted, for I deeply respected Emile and his menu of skills.

Emile's first assignment was to direct *Trailblazers of Modern Dance*, a performance documentary. We wanted to include Frederick Ashton's *Five Brahms Waltzes in the Manner of Isadora Duncan*, with an Ashton favorite, Lynn Seymour. We set up the filming in London. It was a rare privilege to hear Ashton talk about his inspiration to make the piece and then doing it and it was awesome to see Lynn interpret it. Isadora came alive and danced for us.

Dance in America was back to two units: Judy Kinberg became

Emile's associate and Catherine Tatge became mine. Catherine was mightily personable and imaginative with a strong work ethic. She soon became my surrogate daughter.

DIRECTING MERCE CUNNINGHAM

The first thing one learns when you work with Merce is that you do not direct him; you listen to what he wants to do. Merce and I had worked together agreeably on *Camera 3* so *DIA* was a reunion. A friend of mine was the producer for Horowitz's recordings. I once said to him, "You have the most difficult job in the world." He replied, "Not at all, Horowitz's contract says that he can play anything he wants at any time of day or night in any place in the world. My job is easy; I just do what he says."

Working with Merce was something like that. Voices were never raised. He said what he "preferred" to do and what he "preferred" not to do. Very gentlemanly!

Merce insisted his pieces had no story. Watchers just as strongly insisted there was a story and that Merce was holding out on them. Often they thought they saw fragmented story elements and would ask Merce for confirmation. This annoyed him. One day he announced, "Everybody should make up his own story and then we can compare them."

When we were recording Merce's dance, it was difficult for the cameramen because it had no music to hold onto. The dances were recorded with only the natural sound. The sound track would be added later.

After the first rehearsal one of the cameramen slipped into the control room to whisper to me, "There's no music." Our last experience in Nashville had been with Ballet Theater. The camera guys had been spoiled by Copland's *Billy the Kid.* I told him that Merce and his dancers were extraordinarily musical, that they should watch them and see the music. He left, unsatisfied. At that moment I received a call from New York where John Cage was composing the score. The caller said, "You won't believe what he's doing. He's snapping twigs and breaking branches." My instructions were to let John do whatever he damned well wanted.

Merce Cunningham

We edited the program without the track. Girish was especially admiring of the dance and the dancers. Then came the day we added John's track. After a few minutes Girish asked if he could see me in the hall. He was in tears, "Those sounds are spoiling a beautiful show." I told him that's the way it is with Merce and John. I also told him, when he got it home, he could replace the twigs and branches with the Tchaikovsky *Fourth Symphony.*

CLYTEMNESTRA AND MARTHA

During the meeting to choose the program for Martha's first *DIA* program, her associate enthusiastically suggested *Clytemnestra.* Martha snapped him a look and asked, "Do you want to kill them (the audience) off the first year?"

Two years later we were meeting again. Martha had been watching *DIA* and had seen that we were serious and that audiences were accepting it.

She wanted to do *Clytemnestra.* Martha had her instruction, as always: "NO WIDE SHOTS." That was understandable. The year was 1978 and few home television screens were more than twelve inches. As Martha said, "They look like ants," and she was right. That was a challenge for me, but an agreed-upon one.

The theater length of the piece was almost two hours (110 minutes). She asked my opinion and I said, "It should be no longer than one hour and twenty minutes (eighty minutes)." Television needed time for openings and closings etc. She didn't flinch; rather she moved to the piano bench with the composer. I thought she would cut scenes. No! She shortened and trimmed, as with a razor blade, until it was perfect.

She had a friend/writer who wrote for her, but we needed someone to speak the text. Martha wanted British; so we started with the favorite, Laurence Olivier, who was not available and worked our way down the ladder until we found Christopher Plummer, an available and accepting Canadian. During the taping I questioned his flamboyant presentation; he said he "was trying to give it great *panache,*" which I understood meant *a plume of feathers.* I asked if we might have fewer feathers.

The taping went swimmingly because of the dancers and because of Martha's strong support and guidance of me. I think she was pleased and I believe it was the best work I've ever made. She made me better than I could be. And Martha said she wasn't a collaborator?

WORKING WITH BALANCHINE

A year before submitting the *Dance in America* proposal to the National Endowment for the Arts, Jac Venza and Emile Ardolino, who was writing the proposal, contacted various dance companies for permission to list them as possible participants. That included a conversation with Lincoln Kirstein representing the New York City Ballet, who listened then declared that the NYCB "would never appear on anything as vulgar as television." Out! Finished! No Negotiation.

Later, I was hired as Series Producer for *DIA*. At the announcement of the series at the Dance Collection of the New York Public Library at Lincoln Center, we noticed that Barbara Horgan, Balanchine's personal assistant, came and was sitting alone in the back row. I chose to interpret that as an omen. The next day I wrote a letter to Mr. Balanchine telling him that I was the new kid on the block and that it would be unconscionable to call a series *Dance in America* without his participation. I asked to discuss it with him "at his convenience, at any time, any place." I had the note hand delivered.

Next day Barbara called. She laughingly said, "You're very clever. I think I should arrange a lunch for the two of you." I told her, "I deeply appreciate that." She named a date and time and said, "Meet us at Poulailler," a French restaurant on 65th Street that was Balanchine's favorite.

We all arrived together and he was charming. I had determined not to be pushy. He wanted to tell me about his experiences in film and Hollywood. He told me that during the making of *The Goldwyn Follies* in 1938 he'd presented a dance to Mr. Goldwyn by guiding him from one camera to another to see each planned shot through the camera viewfinder. Goldwyn finally asked, "Can't you make a dance that I can see sitting in one place?" He talked about his enthusiasm for the things that film could uniquely do and about the famed Gregg Toland, his cameraman and teacher. His enthusiasm was writ large. Then he wanted to know about me and what I'd done. I told him I had been trained as a pianist and added biographical notes. Finally, he said, "Now, what do you want from me?" I said, "*Dance in America* would like to present, with your collaboration, your ballets." (I had no idea then that collaboration would be the prevailing issue of the series). He answered, "Television is about stories. I don't tell stories; only one story I told *(Prodigal Son)*. You want Tudor; he tells stories."

I feared at this point the relationship was beginning to wobble. I sensed he was beginning to slip away; so I talked about music as storytelling, abstract storytelling; how the sequence of harmonies, the necessity of the chordal patterns, tell a story. I'm not at all sure that I knew what I was talking about, but I was determined to regain his interest, He listened, thought and then said, "Oh, I never thought of it that way." He paused for a moment, then said, "Which ballets would you like to present?" I told him I didn't know. I wanted him to know that I was willing to negotiate. He said, "I'll tell you what: Season is just beginning (it was October); you come anytime you want and see what you like. When you have idea, you come talk to me and we settle." I thought that was fair and generous. Then he asked, "What did you mean 'with your collaboration'?" I explained how we planned to work intimately with each choreographer. He liked that idea.

Later, I learned about his 1973 German experience. Fifteen ballets were assigned to three directors, each with a different style: one with zoom-in, zoom-out; another with continuous panning; the third with spastic editing. Each director had a theory about directing dance. Balanchine might object, but no German is going to compromise his theory; so Balanchine left and came home.

As we were parting, he said, "By the way, how much you know about ballet?" I told the truth, "Nothing." He said, "Good, I teach you."

While watching the entire season, I continually reminded myself of the size of the television screens at that time, usually around twelve inches. With that in mind I went to see him. The first piece I thought would be marvelous on television was the *Melancholic* movement from *The Four Temperaments*; it had a soloist and a quartet of supporting girls. He liked that idea; then, we talked about the second movement (duet with small group) and the third movement (solo with small group). I began to see where he was taking me and I said, "But *Choleric*, the fourth movement, is out of the question. When that crowd of people enters, on television they'll look like a colony of ants." He then made the all-time great comeback, "They don't stay too long;" he then added, "Don't worry, I fix." That was the way we agreed.

He had an incredible sense of tempo on television. He watched it; that's the difference. It's no surprise that choreographers who watched television felt more comfortable preparing dances for television. Merce watched it, Twyla watched and Balanchine watched it. His favorite program was *Wonder Woman*. He saw television as a two-dimensional flat medium. When someone went from downstage to upstage, the illusion is that they are going away. Not to Balanchine, "They are big, then they get small."

The company was already booked and not able to appear on *Dance in America* until our third season. The series was originally scheduled for two seasons. I always thought that Balanchine was the carrot responsible for the extension. *The Four Temperaments* was the first ballet we recorded for that third season. Just before we taped the first theme, he called a halt. "All wrong, all wrong." He went to the floor and refaced the girl of a couple. I asked why and he said, "She is bow-legged. Audience should not see." That's the kind of care and attention he gave to the presentation of his dancers.

When we got to the dreaded fourth movement and all those people appeared, I said, "Maestro"—Balanchine excused himself and went to the floor and stood by the monitor with his pointer finger ready. "Millimeter," he directed, as he repositioned each dancer. When he had finished composing for the screen, he turned to the control room, smiled and said, "See, I fix." He liked the changes he had made and he kept them in the theater version.

Merrill and George Balanchine

The Four Temperaments was the last piece on *Choreography by Balanchine, Part I*, which led off with Maurice Ravel's *Tzigane*, a piece that began with a nine-minute crazy, kooky solo for Suzanne Farrell. Other than believing it was something about gypsies, nobody could fathom what the piece was about. I asked him, "Are you sure you want to start the first program with this piece?" He said, "Yes." No explanation. Suzanne told me it was the first piece he made for her after she rejoined the company in 1976. She said, "I didn't know what was going on, but I told myself that Mr. B had never let me down before; so I just did what he said." Anyone who worked with Balanchine became a believer, became a lemming. If he stepped off the cliff, they would follow without doubt or hesitation. That included me.

My usual way of working was with three isolated cameras and sections no longer than five minutes. If I wanted six cameras, I would repeat the section with different camera tasks. I found it the most efficient way. Balanchine was in the control room with me. I would tell him the shooting plan. His film training had been with a single camera. When he saw three cameras at the same time, it was not easy for him to know the sequence of shots. Later, I sometimes had a problem: if he liked a shot and wanted to use it at a different place than I planned. When that promised to happen, I would tell the subject camera to cap up so he can't see the shot. That happened at the end of *Prodigal Son*. It was a high crane shot that slowly moved down and pushed into Baryshnikov crawling into his father's arms. Balanchine loved that shot and wanted to use it earlier. "Cap up, boys; don't let him see it."

Before working on any piece I would ask Balanchine to tell me everything that related to the piece. I wanted to get inside his head and find his intention. And he would talk. It wouldn't be an analysis of the piece. He might tell me about dating a beautiful Hungarian actress. Then he might tell me about the wallpaper pattern in a London restaurant where they dined. Anything he told me helped me to understand the piece better. "Now, what's *Tzigane* about?" And he told me: "It's a hot night and the girl can't sleep so she comes out of her wagon to cool off. A young man passes by on his way home from the bar. He sees the young girl and wants to get acquainted. They dance. The gypsies pass by; they hear and think it's a party, so they join in. Everybody dances." I got that this dance had humor; many theater audiences didn't get that Balanchine was having fun. On stage there was no setting. I suggested we have one for television to give it a mood. He liked the idea: "Nice, very nice." I also suggested that we could use some film magic; we could make the young man and the gypsies just appear rather than see them run on. "How can you do that?" "By editing. Now you don't see them; now you do." He liked that sort of thing. It was unbelievable to see Balanchine reshape a work in front of me. I had no sense of "Isn't it terrible that he's changing his work." None of that; he was making it better—for television. And he would keep making it better and better.

It was about this time that I became aware that his word of highest praise was "pretty". Sometimes I wasn't as fond of something as he was. When he asked, I'd say, "It's not very pretty." Immediately he would say, "I change." To paraphrase Danilova: "He has so many ideas that they pour like grains of salt."

We did the first two programs, taping them back-to-back in Nashville's Grand Ole Opry. For the second program Balanchine suggested selections from *Jewels*, his masterpiece that highlights the ballet styles of France, America and Russia. *Rubies* (America) and *Diamonds* (Russia) each had a notable pas de deux, but *Emeralds* (France) was not as easy. Balanchine had choreographed it for the singular talents of Violette Verdy who had since retired. Some of her ballets had been withdrawn; others carefully adjusted. For *DIA* he chose a defining opening, a clever duet and a spirited trio.

The finale of the second program was *Stravinsky Violin Concerto*. I resisted it because I could find nothing to do except make a good record tape. I thought there were so many aspects, all simultaneous, that I said, "I can't do anything with it. It doesn't need television interpretation. It doesn't need television." He listened to my complaining then said, "I know. Just, let's do it." He wanted a record on tape. It was an incredible piece with incredible dancing.

Once, Peter Martins came into the control room when Balanchine and I were watching a playback of the third movement, a duet with Peter and Kay Mazzo. Peter watched and said, "That's very good. It's a very good piece. I've never seen it because I'm always dancing it." Balanchine was pleased and modestly thanked Peter, who effusively continued telling him how good he thought the piece was. Finally, Balanchine said, "You want to know how I do it? First I be her; then I be him. You see AC, DC."

Peter Martins and Mr. B.

We taped our third program with NYCB a year later (we usually taped during August when the company was not in season). It was *Chaconne* with Suzanne and Peter and *Prodigal Son* with Baryshnikov. Balanchine had an exceptionally unpleasant working relationship with Prokofiev, who wouldn't cut anything, during the making of *Prodigal*. "It was never right and Prokofiev never changed it." Balanchine never permitted it to be filmed. During our rehearsal Balanchine had never been more alive. It was the first time he and Misha had worked together. The crew had a side bet: "Who will speak Russian first?" It was Misha. He demonstrated everything for Misha, including crawling on his knees and climbing on a table. Misha was shocked and protective. At the final rehearsal he played the father as Misha crawled on his knees and pulled himself into his father's arms. It was extremely moving; I slipped downstairs to ask Barbara Horgan if, perhaps, we could prevail upon Balanchine to play the father. Barbara replied, "It's too late. He was hoping you would ask him, but you didn't."

For our production Balanchine went back to the *Prodigal*'s original costume design by Stravinsky's wife, Vera. Everybody, to a person, hated it. Balanchine appeared not to notice and the costume stayed; Misha never revealed his opinion. Balanchine also became involved in the makeup. He brought in pictures of old Russian icons as models for the face of the father. After four difficult days of taping, we all were spent. As the set was being struck, he and I sat on the side, resting. He said, "We will never have to do this again. I've made it right for Misha."

Martha had made us Prestigious, Balanchine made us Credible. I regarded the two-year extension a bonus as attributable to Mr. B and Martha, our two "Living Treasures". For our fourth year I wanted to present two Balanchine and two Graham programs. Not everybody agreed with me, especially Eliot Feld who rattled around the halls of the National Endowment for the Arts until he was included, which meant cutting one Martha. Emile agreed to direct the Feld program and I went to Japan with Faubion Bowers to film at the Kabukiza in Tokyo.

I was impressed how easily Balanchine could move from the proscenium stage to the television studio; on stage the dominant shape is a rectangle, on television, a triangle. Adjustments needed to be made. We called them translations, a euphemism. The credit became *Choreographed and Reconceived for Television by Balanchine.*

Merrill and Mr. B. in rehearsal

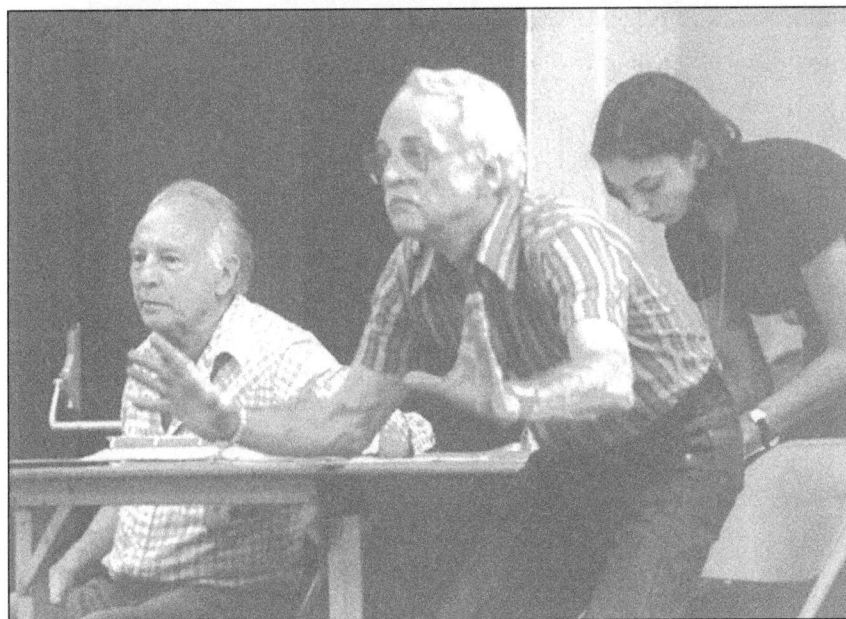

Merrill and Mr. B. in rehearsal

Merrill and Mr. B. in rehearsal

Balanchine liked to see full figures move through space; he liked to see where they started and where they ended. In order to show that, the shot would be wide and the dancers would be tiny. I tightened as much as I could by developing a frame that didn't move, in which the dancer started on one side and ended on the other. The alternative was tracking the dancer through space. Balanchine pointed out, with that choice "Dancers don't move, only scenery moves." That was the dilemma; so each time the situation appeared, I gave him the choice. "Do you want to see them go through space, or do you want to be tighter and see the scenery move? Choreographer's choice."

A similar situation with Martha: She said, "It's too wide; they look like ants." I told her I agreed and said, "Then make me a tighter shot." And she would. Same thing with a close-up: Martha was enthralled with the beauty of Takako Asakawaya's face. At one point in *Diversion of Angels* Martha asked, "Could you make a close-up there?" I said, "If you choreograph it, I'll take it." She immediately understood that close-ups are not made from whimsy, they are designed. I determined that, in any situation, I must maintain the integrity of the choreography without arguing with the choreographer. Stage works will not work on television without adjustments. That was the reason I hated directing live broadcasts. Fortunately, Emile enjoyed doing them.

As a procedure, during rehearsal and in coordination with the dancers, I would take Balanchine from camera to camera showing him the sequence of shots I proposed. (I didn't realize until later, but I was putting him through the Goldwyn adventure). If he came to something and said, "I don't know about this," I would say, "Do you want the picture wider or tighter? The camera, higher or lower? To the right or to the left?" Television is a primitive medium: the language is limited and there are only so many letters in the alphabet. He would say, "Show me," and the cameraman would present alternate choices. Most of the times he accepted the original with, perhaps, a Balanchinean refinement. Any changes he suggested were improvements, He never suggested rearranging a sequence, which was a relief, since that can play havoc with camera rotation.

There is always a lot of waiting around in a television studio. Technicians are forever adjusting lights and fussing with cameras. If we were not involved, Balanchine and I would sit in an out-of-the-way spot. Often we were silent, watching. Then he would turn to me and start telling me something, I called them his little essays. I interpreted them, as "This is something you need to know." For example, he might talk about why, in dancing, a step is not equal to a note; then he would talk about steps and notes. The most memorable thing he told me was: "Dancing is not the steps; it's in-between the steps." That totally changed my viewing perceptions, but I couldn't understand how some dancers were mechanically "doing steps" and others appeared to be dancing. And then, I had the privilege of attending an *Interpreter's Archive* recording of the original dancer coaching a particular role with a younger NYCB dancer.

I viewed two episodes with Maria Tallchief and a young dancer and I learned about dancing between the steps.

Barbara Horgan told me later that he enjoyed talking music with me. He had many people who wanted to talk dancing with him. One day he showed me what he had done in making *A Midsummer Night's Dream*. He was proud that the music was only Mendelssohn; he wanted no composed transitions. It had taken him ten years to fit all the pieces together.

It's often mentioned, but not emphasized enough, what an extraordinary musician he was. He was trained first as a musician, then a dancer. Every piece he choreographed is a testimony to his musical training. In recording sessions he knew what he wanted and insisted. He knew, as Merce knew, that music must be faster on television than in the theater. We don't know why; it's just an electronic fact. The saying is, "One real minute will seem like four television minutes." Merce's *Rainforest* plays twenty-four minutes on stage; on television he moved it along to nineteen minutes. He knew.

Our collaboration was strengthened because of Balanchine's confidence in the crew. We trained that crew and it was always the same people. We began in Nashville with two cameramen from New York and one from Nashville. Soon, all were from Nashville. They were extraordinarily skilled craftsmen. I continued to use them on every project I did until I retired. And they were trained by the Balanchine experience.

At one point during our first lunch Balanchine looked at me and asked, "But would you trust the dancing?" I, of course, said I would. At that time I was not totally aware of what he meant. He told me that, in the past, he had not supervised the transfer of his dances to television, that he leased out his pieces to *The Ed Sullivan Show* and *The Bell Telephone Hour* because the company needed money and the dancers needed work. He also said he was not always pleased with the treatment his dances received. "Now," he said, "we don't need money so we don't lease out." As we worked together I began to understand that he was talking about respect for the dance and the dancers.

Twyla Tharp, also, was a protector of dance. She would ask, "Did you make that edit for dance reasons, musical reasons, or personal reasons?

Because the dancing doesn't need it." A visual sequence for television is usually an arrangement of wide, medium and tight shots. Each category is necessary to give variety and avoid monotony. The close-up is a television favorite. The problem with dancing, Balanchine especially, is that the full-body view is the tight shot and anything tighter is a specialty shot. A further problem is that television audiences are captivated by the face shot. Balanchine dancing is not about faces. We watched and learned that not all Balanchine dancing was necessarily full-body view. A lot of the dancing was face and arms so we developed the port-de-bras shot. When the legs and thighs were not intimate with the dancing, I could move in and cut off the lower part of the body. By the same token, shots of the feet and legs alone were never acceptable. I learned that to trust the dancing was not so easy. British television leaders found my work "boring". They wanted more "Pizzazz".

When, at the end of our first meeting, Mr. B asked me how much I knew about ballet and I told him "nothing" and he replied, "Good. I teach you." I had no idea what that meant. When we began to work together, it became clear that nothing in his working life was off-limits to me. I could watch classes, rehearsals and performances and he was always open for questions and explanations. From my observances I began to understand his ways of working. First: If he was teaching, the instruction was always succinct and quietly given. When he was watching the execution, his attention was always focused. His comments were always quietly and personally given. In short, he was a man who knew what he wanted to see and how to quietly communicate it.

These Balanchine observations lay quietly within me until I retired to Santa Fe and met Catherine Oppenheimer, a former NYCB dancer and became her friend. I watched her set up the National Dance Institute of New Mexico, which has become an arts treasure in impoverished New Mexico. I became aware that, in working situations, we always agreed. Catherine's way of working was Balanchine's.

Years later when, with the collaboration of the Lensic Performing Arts Center in Santa Fe, I was presenting ballet companies and I invited Suzanne Farrell and her company. When she was dancing and I was directing, we worked together several times. This time she was the leader. I watched classes, rehearsals and coaching sessions. It was pure Balanchine.

All the time that the system of shooting was evolving, so was the approach to editing. That was because I was blessed to be working with Emile and Girish Bhargava. I don't think the importance of editing can be overemphasized, especially the system that Girish, Emile and I evolved. Girish was our leader. He was a very musical person. He didn't have musical training, but he was natively musical. I am convinced that editing must be musical. If you don't believe me, just observe the television screen today and see what passes for editing. It took some time to learn exactly at which point the edit should happen. After all, there are thirty frames to a second; on which frame is the edit? Many directors, too many, dissolve at that point and smear over the edit point because they haven't figured it out. We regarded the dissolve as a specialty shot. Balanchine was instrumental in helping us answer the question, "On which frame do you edit?" He gave us the rule: at the bottom of the breath. For example: inhale, exhale (edit), inhale, exhale (edit) and so on. The edit pushes the shot off. We never cut in the middle of the breath, always at the bottom. Of course, dancers are not universally musical, but they still breathe— sometimes.

Girish had a saying about editing: "With drama and opera the edit can be here or even there, but with dance it should not only be perfect but very perfect." In order to make it very perfect we would determine the edit point, then check it at least three different times. In editing, we found that the body responds differently at different times of day. If you've been drinking, you respond differently and also, if you're tired. And so we checked edits only the first thing in the morning when we were fresh.

I wanted all the programs to look as if they were sired by the same father. That was the reason for developing "The System", which was a series of guidelines for choosing and analyzing a piece, learning the piece and preparing a script, breaking the piece into shorter sections for rehearsing and taping, developing shot possibilities, care and feeding of the cameramen, collaborating with the choreographer and re-conceiving the piece for television. Once the materials had been made, a director's individuality would come forward by the way he or she used them.

Of course, there was a system for recording. Before each shooting day we had a camera conference to show the cameramen the tape of the day's dance—which had been made in rehearsal—and to give the shot sheets and explain their tasks. A task was the assignment within any dance section; each section might have several assignments for each camera. We reminded them of the basic rules: Frame tight but don't cut appendages; lead the dancer, don't follow; don't place the dancer in the center of the picture, rather maintain the dancer at the bottom of the frame, dancing on a sliver of floor; execute smooth zooms that don't bump at the beginning or end; take the tempo of the zoom from the tempo of the dancing; maintain a fluid, breathing frame. Also, before the recording check all viewfinders to confirm that they match corresponding monitors and are marked for broadcast cutoff. This was not necessarily important for drama or opera, but it was vital for dance.

I have observed the career of Peter Boal who joined the NYCB later in the year that Balanchine died. Peter was too late for *Dance in America*, but we worked together on *Essays in the Balanchine Style*. He was a mightily impressive classical dancer. Later, when his interest included contemporary work with his own adjunct group, I invited him to the Lensic. Alas for me, The Pacific Northwest Ballet invited Peter to be their new director. I was delighted for his opportunity and called to congratulate the retiring director, Francia Russell. "Merrill, there was no other." Peter agreed to an appearance with members of his new company and his NYCB partner Wendy Whelan at the Lensic. It was Peter's last appearance as a dancer and he dedicated it to the Santa Fe dance audience and me. That was 2005 and I wasn't able to arrange a further appearance because of Peter's success in Seattle.

Finally, in 2008 we were able to schedule two performances in October, with a conversation between Peter and me the night before. I watched Peter give his group a class, a rehearsal and a class for NDI. Balanchine was alive and at work. We had hoped to open with Robbins' *Fancy Free*, but it was a budget buster and we substituted *In the Night*,

Robbins' first piano ballet for NYCB. We then wanted two Balanchine masterpieces: *Jewels* and *Agon*. I had done this program under Balanchine's supervision on *DIA*: selections from *Emeralds* and a pas de deux each from *Rubies* and *Emeralds*. *Agon* was the ballet I was proudest to present at the Lensic. For me, it was Balanchine's answer to young choreographers who announce they would "expand the boundaries of ballet." Balanchine, in *Agon*, was saying, "If that's what you want, I'll show you how." That's *Agon*, as fresh in 2008 as it was when it was choreographed in 1957. The Santa Fe audience had never heard about it, but they watched and stood up and cheered. I felt warmed.

Other choreographers develop designs and plans in their heads and then select dancers to execute those plans. (I also found that many choreographers were not too interested in scenic design and some were cavalier about lighting—not true with Paul Taylor who, during the rehearsal process, would ask, "When does Jennie (Jennifer Tipton) arrive?" Balanchine was different: he would have an idea that included characters; he would select dancers who had the individual possibility of growing into a full character. For me, it was like selecting a plant, caring for it and watching it grow. When Suzanne brought her dancers to Santa Fe, my memory of Balanchine's process was reaffirmed; when her dancers told me that she didn't want the dancer doing her role to do it the way she did. She wanted each one to find her own individuality.

All this has given me great hope and assurance: if you have a message that you've thought through and believe in and then present it clearly and simply without drama, it will be heard, listened to and remembered.

MORE GUIDANCE FROM BALANCHINE:
I once asked Mr. B:

Q: "How do you get an audience's attention and hold it?"
A: "When the curtain opens, a person or a small group doing something must draw the audience's attention. Let nothing or nobody interfere with the audience's focus on that person or

group. When he, she or they exit, the next person or group enters from the same side and that is the procedure that continues; no one enters from the opposite side of the exit. That keeps the audience's focus intact."

Balanchine shared his suite of two offices with Jerry Robbins. Jerry had to walk through Balanchine's office to get to his. Several times Balanchine and I would be talking and Jerry entered to get to his office. I thought it curious that he didn't greet us and walk across the floor, but he didn't: he would enter, without greeting and silently follow the walls to his office.

One day I got a call from Barbara that Balanchine wanted to talk to me. We met and he told me that Jerry had been aware of our conferences and had seen our programs and that he was becoming interested in doing television. Mr. B said, "You must not direct. Jerry always has to have a scapegoat—and it would be you." I was deeply moved and thanked him for his concern.

And Jerry <u>was</u> interested. *DIA* was planning a program of two duets. Peter Martins had agreed to do one, Jerry agreed to the other. Jerry's was a lovely duet for Makarova and Baryshnikov. I suggested to Emile that he direct Jerry's duet and he agreed; I produced. Jerry followed Martha's method of "requests"; he wanted it filmed (not videotaped) in a theater (not a studio). That was only the beginning of his requests Emile took care of it gracefully, which gave me time to look around. I looked into a studio where Makarova was warming up. As I remember, her young baby was in a basket on the floor; she was at the barre with a sandwich in one hand and a cigarette in the other. She was as nonchalant about my appearance as she was when Jerry stepped in. We watched as she mesmerized us: she moved from a flat foot—slowly, slowly to *en pointe* and, without stopping, then slowly, slowly back to flat. I was breathless; Jerry started tearing up and saying, "I've never seen anything like that before." That was Jerry's lovable side. Later, when Emile had hit a Jerry snag, he and I were talking about it in the lobby as Jerry walked by muttering, "You guys are amateurs!"

KATHERINE DUNHAM

During 1979 I began thinking about the next *DIA* project to be broadcast in 1980. Black companies had been represented on the series by Dance Theatre of Harlem and it had been a delight to work with Arthur Mitchell and his beautifully behaved and talented company

As usual we took the company to Nashville. During the rehearsal and taping, the flies were crowded with stagehands peering over the railings. I assumed it was to see how these black people would behave. I knew how Arthur trained his dancers and I further knew that their behavior would be acceptable for an audience with the Queen. And it was.

I wanted a program of black dance to reflect its history. That decided, there was only one candidate for me: Katherine Dunham.

Catherine Tatge was producing; she called Miss Dunham (and she would always be Miss Dunham to me) who was pleased, but said that we would have to prepare and record the program in Haiti where she then lived.

Catherine and I flew to Haiti to research the situation. We found that it would be difficult for Catherine to mingle because Haiti was a troubled foreign country and everyone we met wanted to come to America and each one was sure we could arrange it.

The meetings with Miss Dunham were cordial and boded well for our return with the crew. Catherine did yeoman service of transporting, feeding and housing the crew and their equipment, but on an errand, she had an unfortunate accident: she stepped into a plump cow patty. A city official saw the incident and came to her rescue. He took her to his office, took off her shoe and washed her feet. Chivalry was not dead in Haiti.

When taping began, I did the interview with Miss Dunham, who was most forthcoming and generous. I was fascinated by her account of her illustrious history. When I had a live subject, I often liked to ask a final question: "What message would you like on your tombstone?" I was especially touched by Miss Dunham's answer: "*She tried.*"

The performances would be in two parts: selections from her dances, which I thought historically important and would be taped later in Nashville with her original dancers and the performance of what she called, *Voodon* and the dictionary calls voodoo, a black religious cult practiced in the Caribbean and the southern U.S., combining elements of Roman Catholic ritual with traditional African magical and religious rites and characterized by sorcery and spirit possession. Miss Dunham was a Grand Mambo in that tradition and had her own performance space. When she showed it to me, she asked, "Do you think Americans are ready to meet a Mambo and see a ceremony?" I admitted that I didn't know, but "I think we're going to find out."

The ceremony began: Miss Dunham was on her throne. A male Mambo led the ceremony. I soon learned that a continuing flow of rum was a part of it and the male Mambo was a frequent imbiber. As I was directing the activities, I noticed that something unexplained was happening around Miss Dunham. She handled it skillfully and I could return to including her. Afterward, I learned that the male Mambo was drunk and tried to kill her, an attempt she parried.

The broadcast of the program happened while an unfortunate incident between America and Haiti occurred. I think it involved illegal immigrants. Jack Gould of the *New York Times* scolded me and many viewers agreed with him. Contrarily, many viewers saw what I was trying to do. I was proud of the program, but I never thought that this would be the last program I would direct for *DIA* as on-staff director.

Last Words about My Mother

On the late years of the 1970s my mother was invited by her brother, a recent widower, to share his winter residence in Tampa, Florida. She accepted and soon found that she liked it as long as she could go home in springtime to plant and care for her garden. I liked the arrangement because Florida was much easier for me to visit from New York than Indiana; so I visited her several times a year. On one trip she told me that her last physical exam had revealed that she had leukemia, but that it was slowing-burning and not life threatening—if she took care of it. Come spring and she went to Indiana with doctor instructions. Now, what happened has two versions: mine from New York and cousin Betty's from nearby in southern Michigan. Since the Indiana doctor was 30+ miles away, I thought that she had been careless about going. Betty's version was that she had gone, but the doctor didn't like the Florida doctor's advice and substituted his own. Whatever the reason, by autumn she was weak and desperately ill and wanted to go back to Florida. She complicated her return by refusing an available $350 first-class airfare, "That's too much to pay," (training from the Great Depression never completely fades away). This was a serious delay, but when her return was finally arranged, it was with sizable physical support. Once there she presented herself to her doctor; he examined and told her, "You waited too long;" and placed her in a hospital.

I flew to see her, and it was clear she was aware she was dying. She said to me, "I always thought you would go before me." I'm sure she thought I had my father's lifeline (died at fifty-seven, with all his family dead before him) rather than hers (mother died at 100, brother at 102, twin sister at 105).

The rest of my visit was about my learning her financial and funeral plans; they were extensive. On Christmas Day, I arrived at the hospital, and we were speaking together when her lunch was served. I think she was embarrassed because she was eating alone. She said, "I expect you'll want to go home now." I recognized my cue to leave.

In New York, on New Year's Eve I received a call from my uncle. My mother was dead; she was eighty-one. Later, another call, this time from the woman who was preparing her body for shipment to Indiana. She told me that she was placing her wedding ring on one of her toes. I was non-plussed and asked "Why?" I'll never forget her reply: "To thwart train robbers."

I flew to Indiana for the funeral. My mother was a member of the *Order of the Eastern Star*, which, I believe, is the female version of the male *Masons*. There was a ritual ceremony by the members at the funeral home. All I remember is that the hem of every lady's skirt was crooked.

At the church my mother had planned every detail of the funeral: participants, hymns, Biblical passages for the sermon. As I listened, I felt tyranny from the grave. Aunt Lydia and I emptied the attic and the house, guided by meticulous instructions. The house was a showplace in the town. For that I received a rousing $34,000 in1980.

I was driven to the airport in South Bend. That was my last time in New Carlisle, and I plan no further visits.

1980—1982

*T*he beginning of my departure from *Dance in America* was Jac Venza's announcement that Bob Joffrey was offering his company's production of *Nijinsky* with Rudolph Nureyev to *DIA*. I was first surprised, then dismayed. I told Jac that *DIA* enjoyed the trust of its viewers; we had never presented anything or anyone that we didn't believe was the best. That Nureyev's career was over and had been for several years, was an open secret in the dance world. I volunteered to make a documentary, celebrating Nureyev's accomplishments; but said, "His present dancing is not acceptable." Jac was adamant and his final statement insured my leaving, "We will find something else for you to do."

Unexpectedly, at the same time I received a call from my former boss at CBS, Bob Shay, who wanted to take me to lunch to tell me that CBS was starting a cable channel, an arts channel and that he had been appointed the leader. He then asked me to be as much a part of it as my time would allow. I responded with, "How about full time?" He was delighted and asked what title I wanted: "Executive Producer of Arts Programs". He agreed and I was back at CBS. He added, "Merrill, I've always loved your work, but I don't know how you do it; so do what you do—just don't bore me."

Soon enough, Jack Willis became the Program Director and my immediate superior. I was delighted: I respected Jack's integrity and work as a documentary filmmaker. There was an unexpected sidelight to Jack's coming to CBS CABLE: he didn't come cheap. Bob Shay revised my contract to reflect a better balance with Jack's salary. Bob Shay was a gentleman; not at all the model of a major corporate executive.

During my early days, Jack took me to meetings at Black Rock (corporate headquarters) where I experienced Mister Paley and the men of middle management (remember The Suits from *Camera 3* days). I had to relearn how to tie a tie and wear a jacket. Mister Paley was an enthusiast for the new CBS CABLE. I was impressed by his alertness. He knew the right questions to ask and he persisted until he was satisfied. Later he was quoted as announcing, "At last, we've done something right."

But there was something we didn't do right and it was his goof. He insisted that CBS CABLE be a sponsored service. Soon enough it became clear that we should look to the future rather than the past and be a pay service. Later, it would become evident that The Suits did not share Paley's enthusiasm. Where this would take us was not clear—yet.

I was proud of the staff assembled:

- Roger Englander: an honored television director for his musical programs, including Leonard Bernstein's *Young Person's Concerts*. Roger replaced me at *Camera 3*, when I left.
- Glenn Dubose: my first associate director when I came to CBS, who left to teach at a northern California college; now returned with expanded dramatic arts experience.
- Glenn Berenbeim: my assistant and a recent graduate from

Harvard, who brought youth, enthusiasm and a desire to be a writer.

- Julia Hays: also a recent graduate of Harvard and the daughter of the brilliant scenic designer, David Hays. Julia kept the office and me together, with her charm and organizational skills.
- Later, they would be joined by John Musilli; as drama coordinator.

Roger and I spent a week in Munich looking at a library of European materials to see what we could lease. Nulla! A lot of the shows were looking old fashioned. Contrary to prevailing European thought, there are not a lot of evergreens in art. Look at *A&E* with their BBC library. Art programs reflect the time in which they were made.

I was proud of the product we produced. The gossip on the street was that we were spending a lot of money. But we were right on our business plan. The question asked was: "Will you make money?" The answer was, "Yes, as a quality boutique; no, as Macy's." In fact, I wore a tee shirt that announced, "QUALITY COSTS." We began to see the audience response: it was not the eighteen to forty-five group that the networks hunger for; but, rather, a well educated one: fifty and older, better educated and wealthier; which today is the audience ignored by the networks.

In those days I wasn't directing because CBS CABLE had no contract with the unions; so I began developing a list of non-union directors. Most of them were British who wanted to come to America; a few—very few—were young and promising Americans. Gary Halvorson was among the few. Gary had been trained as a pianist. I had known him as a production assistant at WNET and believed he should have an opportunity to explore his talents. I persuaded JacVenza to let him be a part of a two-month dance/video summer workshop that I was then conducting at Duke University. At CBS CABLE, Gary was chief contributor to one of our accomplishments: recording the immediacy of chamber music. When it's televised in a proscenium situation, it looks removed and feels aloof. We moved the musicians into a studio for greater control and into a circle facing each other for greater intimacy. We also emphasized variety: of musicians and instruments, of periods of music, of instrumental combinations. The sections were short, which gave a faster tempo to the shows.

Jack Willis was especially supportive. He and I were an empathetic duo. There were few taste differences; besides, Jack and I trusted each other. Also, there were few money problems. I had been trained to make my shows with minimal money. Now we had more and we could let out our imaginations. This was one of the best periods in my life.

I was proud of the productions, especially:

- *Kennedy's Children* with Shirley Knight recreating her Tony Award-winning role for television. (I directed. The union contracts had been signed.)
- *Sizwe Banzi is Dead*, by the South African playwright, Athol Fugard and performed by the Tony Award-winning cast. (I directed.)
- *Paris, I Love You* with Zizi Jeanmaire and Roland Petit's Ballet National de Marseilles, which was videotaped in Paris. (I directed.)
- *Confessions of a Cornermaker* by choreographer Twyla Tharp, which won a 1982 Ace Award for Innovative Programming. (Twyla directed, I produced.)

A footnote about this program: I had directed two programs with Twyla. The first was for *Camera 3*—so dreadful that, "I buried it so deep, that even hogs, snorting for truffles, couldn't find it." The second, for *Dance in America*, was acceptable, but not my finest hour. For *Confessions*, I invited Twyla to direct it; as she knew television and how to make translations from the stage. She didn't know how to use three cameras in recording; so I arranged for the cameramen to teach her. Her friend, Jerry Robbins, told her she had ruined the piece. I thought it was the best-directed dance that I had ever seen on television. I added: "And I, as Executive Producer, hired her."

Davidsbündlertänze by Balanchine, with principals from the New York City Ballet, deserves a footnote too. I had directed three *Choreography by Balanchine* programs for *DIA*. They had been rich experiences for me and, I think, for Balanchine—he liked that I had musical training. When I told him about my new venture, I said that my new budgets would not be able to accommodate the costs of the NYCB orchestra contract. Two years later I got a call from Barbara Horgan: "He wants to talk with you. He has an idea." That idea was *Davidsbündlertänze* with only a solo piano and a limited number of principal dancers. I could afford that and we made preparations. *Davidsbündlertänze* was one of Balanchine's last works and some people believe that it has the aura of "goodbye" about it. We taped, as usual, in Nashville using the big stage rather than the studio.

There was distance between the stage and the control room; so we arranged a golf cart to transport him and me; as it appeared that his physical powers were diminished. The cart was used only once; it embarrassed him and he preferred to walk; so we walked and talked together, mostly about the piece. Balanchine never had program notes to inform about the dance. As a former musicology student, I had learned about the Schumann legend; so I asked him whether it might be helpful for an audience to know the Robert and Clara love story of the dance. He heartily agreed and I began thinking how I could use the information in the television program. I also asked him about his decision to use the story. His reply: "Lincoln (Kirstein) left a copy of the score outside my door."

There was one event during the taping of the double duet: I had blocked it as two duets. During rehearsal he stopped and said to me, "No, it is a double duet." Time out, while I re-thought and re-blocked.

By fall of 1982, I was in Paris taping the Ballet National de Marseilles, when a surprising incident occurred. In preparation for shooting I had asked and it was agreed, that I would have, a crane on the first day of shooting. The day arrived, the crane didn't. The French attitude was to make do another way. I had been promised; so I said, "I will wait for the promised crane." We waited the whole day. That night I was not sure I had done the right thing; so I asked my producer, Catherine Tatge, to ask her father, an American Consul in Paris. His answer: "You did the right thing. They may be northern, but they're still Latin."

The taping was concluding when I got a call from Jack Willis in New York: "Stay there, don't come home. There's too much blood flowing here." Mister Paley was retired and The Suits had cancelled CBS CABLE. Now we knew. They really didn't want it. But they never replaced it with anything else. Today CBS is not on cable and The Suits have scattered.

The loss was an estimated fifty million dollars. We couldn't believe that any group of executives would make such a draconian decision. We knew, by that time, that we should be a pay-channel, but contracts with cable operators for five years wouldn't permit that. The game plan was that we would begin to turn a profit after three years. I swear, to our understanding, we were right on schedule. There was a lot of talk on the street about the money we were spending, but not much about many of our programs beginning to sell. That was because Regina Dantes, our beautiful Brazilian Bombshell, was in charge of acquisitions and co-productions. Because of her, Europe was beginning to buy our programs. Although we couldn't prove it, we believed that quality could sell—like a quality boutique.

1983

O was about to become sixty and for the first time in thirty years I was unemployed. No stranger came forward, so I could not depend on the kindness of strangers—but a friend did. Judy Kinberg became Senior Producer of *Dance in America* after Emile left for Hollywood. She was loyal and remembering and invited me to direct projects.

Magic Flute

The first was Peter Martins' *Magic Flute* for NYCB. It was a vulnerable time for Peter and for me: Balanchine was dying down the street at Roosevelt Hospital. We sat in his old office, tearful and wondered what he would tell us to do as each crisis threatened. He had already told us and we found that out.

A Song for Dead Warriors

The second project was with an old friend

from *Romeo and Juliet* days, Michael Smuin, who had choreographed a controversial ballet for his company, The San Francisco Ballet, based on the American Indian takeover of Alcatraz. San Francisco audiences were divided between love and hate. Some performances ended with audience members spitting at each other. Judy and I liked that it was a company outside of New York; we liked that the subject was topical and not a fairytale prince in love. Michael had taken ballet language into contemporary life.

We wanted to do it, but there wasn't money to take the dancers to Nashville and do the usual *DIA* production. In addition the stage scenery was a foreground scrim with projections. The dance was behind the scrim. The scrim is a theater device, it doesn't transfer to television. Then I had an idea: if we taped the dance in a black box, the viewer couldn't tell where he is and what the scale is until the defining element is added. That could be done by building real sets and having the dancers perform in real space, or it could be by superimposing selected slides during editing. The latter is what we did and it saved a lot of money and made this production possible. It was amateur Hollywood special effects, but it worked.

A Song for Dead Warriors was not a masterpiece. It was not *Four Temperaments*; it was not *Clytemnestra*. It was a child who wanted to be good, wanted to be liked. I nurtured that child and I also won an Emmy, the only Emmy I won for directing.

China

The China Film Association invited members of the Directors Guild of America to tour China, meet and talk with Chinese filmmakers. Emile joined me and we flew to Beijing, where I remember the absence of automobiles, the streets teeming with bicycles at rush hour, smog, cloudless skies and poverty housing. The Chinese filmmakers had many more government restrictions than we did; they had many questions about that. But we also saw the Great Wall, X'ian with its terracotta soldiers and finally Shanghai, even then, the most westernized of China's cities.

1984

Balanchine died in 1983 from a mystery illness, not defined for two years. We immediately began to prepare a two-part biography, one hour each. Judy Kinberg produced this labor of love. Her research, with the aid and support of Nancy Lassalle, a longtime friend of the NYCB, was remarkable. Lost film footage was found in an attic in Ireland of Balanchine, himself, dancing. Judy also insisted that we bring the out-takes of *Serenade* from Germany so that we could re-edit a section. We found that it had been released out of sync; so Rosemary Dunleavy, the ballet mistress, came in to bring the dancers and the music together.

While we were editing, I felt Balanchine was always up in the corner of the editing room ceiling watching and helping us to be better than we were. We all drew from our memories of him: Judy, Girish and Holly Brubach, who was our writer. We had abundant material and Holly was instrumental in structuring all of it. I thought the first hour was terrific, but I wish I had had more time for fine-tuning the second hour (I don't know why I was being pushed for time and I don't know why I let myself be pushed). After a preview of the programs I received a hand-written, hand-delivered letter:

> *The two sections of the film on Mr. B are a wonderful achievement and you are to be warmly congratulated on its beauty, tact and ingenuity. It is marvelously edited and the cutting and impositions are so very skillfully conceived. I think he would have loved it.*
>
> *Gratefully,*
>
> *Lincoln Kirstein*

AN AUSTRALIAN INVITATION

I was invited to visit Australia as the guest of the Australian Ballet, by its new director, Maina Gielgud. I knew Maina from the 1970s, when I was working with the Bejart Company in Belgium. She was a dancer in the company and a colleague of my friend, Dyane Gray, whom I knew from the Philadelphia Dance Academy. Dyane choreographed the first dance piece I directed on television.

Later, Bejart released Maina, much to her dismay. Maurice said, "for her own betterment." I believed him and the future proved him right. But, Maina was bereaved and spent time with me as I tried to console her.

Maina was a proper English girl—her uncle was John Gielgud—but she was a strong lady and her strength returned in force. She applied for and was appointed artistic director of the ballet company based in Melbourne. She invited and paid for, my trip to assess the video possibilities of the company. I found that the company and the society were too provincial and not ready for any of my ideas. But the trip gave me the opportunity to visit the Great Barrier Reef, one of the unique experiences of my life. I also enjoyed Sydney, the harbor and the design of that extraordinary Opera House, with an unusual exterior, but a skimpily designed back stage.

1985

 $\mathcal{I}$ was introduced to an executive of a fund-raising company. We talked and he told me about his current project, a $50,000,000 capital fund drive for the renovation of Carnegie Hall. I think he liked our conversation because he commissioned me to make a film to aid in the fund raising—"no longer than twelve minutes."

I asked Catherine Tatge to work with me and we began research. Soon, I was astonished at the amount of material found—events, occasions, musical performances (including Judy Garland and Benny Goodman) and more. I organized and selected and went to Girish for editing. At the end, we both agreed it was a beautiful piece of work. But, it was fifteen minutes long.

I presented it to the deciding group with an explanation of the rich body of possibilities. The response, without viewing, was, "It's too long." I had no idea how much three minutes inhibited fund-raising. Then, I became angry—and eloquent: I talked about the rich body of material; then explained my decisions. The deciding group viewed it, liked it and approved it.

Then, I learned of the second part of my assignment: to accompany a fund-raiser, with a VCR player and the tape, to a prospective funder. I became aware that most of them were on, or in the vicinity of, Wall Street. The procedure was: enter, introduce tape, "We brought a tape to remind you of the many joyful occasions you and your wife (or perhaps your wife) have had at Carnegie Hall." None of them looked to me as if he had ever been in Carnegie Hall, or even knew where it was or what it did.

The pitch proceeded in earnest: the machine, the tape and I were dismissed. I learned later that there would be no begging and no taking what they might offer. Extensive research preceded the meeting and the giver was told what he was expected to give.

Whatever the procedure, it worked. $50,000,000 was raised and Carnegie Hall was saved and renovated.

During the preparation I met and interviewed Issac Stern, who was the bulldozer behind the renovation. He also was a friend of Agnes de Mille's husband. We met later at an Agnes dinner party. I learned to like his passion. I never mentioned that I knew about the interchange he had with conductor Eugene Ormandy: "Issac, save Carnegie Hall. But if you don't practice, you can't play with the Philadelphia Orchestra."

1986

Jack Willis was engaged by NBC to be the Executive Producer of a five-part series *Phil Donahue Examines the Human Animal*. I was available and Jack invited me to join him to produce and direct, "as many as you can." I was delighted to be back with Jack and, from our past, I was confident I could do all five. Then I was hit by the tsunami: Phil, the committee, criticism, opinions, suggestions and instructions. I ended by completing only one of the series, *Love and Sex*.

I learned that the network's thinking didn't like or want what I do; contrarily, rarely do I want to watch what they do. I can raise my anger for the ways they have dumbed television down. I am glad that Pat Weaver cannot see the fiasco that television has become. It was not always so.

1987

*T*his was a banner year for me. I directed *Agnes, the Indomitable de Mille*, which was awarded a 1987 Emmy for Outstanding Informational Special. Only the producer receives the award. I was the director and I knew that it was my show for reasons you will read about soon, so I made my own award.

The Agnes story began the day Emile Ardolino, Judy Kinberg and I moved into the *Dance in America* office. Agnes was the first phone caller; it was for Emile, whom she knew, I believe, through his friendship with the Joffrey Company. Agnes was offering herself as a candidate for our series. Emile reported and I was not impressed. I had my list of greats: Balanchine, Graham, Cunningham, Tudor, etcetera and Agnes was not on it. "Later!" Periodically her name would come up and I would repeat, "Later." I had met her by this time and when we met at occasions, we would both nod politely. One night my friend, Marge Champion and I were at an

American Ballet Theatre performance and saw Agnes in a wheelchair. Marge said, "If you're going to do anything with Agnes, you might want to get about it." That night the idea clicked with me and I hired Marge, who was friendly with Agnes, to be a consultant for the project. I think it was Judy Kinberg who had an initial conversation with Agnes to tell her of our intentions and to hold her at bay. Marge and I went to work to look at all of the Agnes material that had been recorded. After a number of hours of viewing, it happened; at the same time we turned to each other and said, "It's not very good choreography," and the problem was exposed.

I went into a blue funk—what to do? I talked with Jack Willis, who always gave me good advice and he said, "You'd best find a reason that you believe in for doing the project, or don't do it." A reason? I had read much of Agnes's plethora of autobiographical writing and I began to see an image: a runner who knocks down the hurdle, gets up, runs, knocks down the second hurdle, gets up, runs, knocks down the third hurdle, etc. I began to build the show with that image. Since she was so articulate, I didn't want a narrator. I decided to interview her myself and I devised the questions. She was open and responsive to me. As for the choreography, she answered my reserve when she talked about her success on Broadway. She said, "I wasn't the best choreographer, but..."

Two notable incidents: Early on I knew how dear the family's summer house was to her and to fit one of her narratives, I filmed the dining room curtains lightly blowing in the wind; it was a mood shot. For the final cut, there was time for either that shot or Agnes talking about begging for a $50 raise for *Oklahoma*. Judy insisted upon that and I was a wimp and gave in. When Agnes saw the finished film, she asked, "Where are the dining room curtains?" The other incident was during her telling of the separation and divorce of her parents after she had graduated from college. "My father had discovered sex;" then he demeaned the mother Agnes adored by calling her "only a housekeeper." Agnes teared up. Later she asked what I had done about it; I told her, "I kept it in."

Agnes loved my representation of her and, I think, with the possible exception of Martha Graham's *Clytemnestra*, it's the best work I did. The happy part is that we became friends. She would invite me for social dinners at her apartment on 8th Street ("but don't wear your rompers"). Those were the days that, informally, I was wearing jump suits. Then there were times she would call and say, "Let's have lunch," and I would travel down and wheel her to the next-door restaurant and we would talk. I loved to talk to her about memories, both hers and mine and about ideas and perceptions that were hers, mine and ours. One day I was talking and she said, "Oh, Merrill, I am not an intellectual."

My sadness is that Agnes didn't protect her legacy. She gave her works to her only son, a professor at a Georgia university. I believe that he was sonly (made-up word), but I don't think he knew what to do with it. And I don't see any evidence that Ballet Theatre does either. History is like Kleenex these days—needed and disposable.

The Central Ballet of China

The other event for me in 1987 was to make a performance-documentary about The Central Ballet of China during their tour of the US. Catherine Tatge was the mover and shaker of this project and she involved me. The back-story: Sidney, a man with financial resources, had married a Chinese wife with culture and they were supporters of The Central Ballet of China from Beijing. Sidney wanted to document their tour in America. He would finance it and said how much he was willing to spend. Catherine and I conferred and told him he was about $100,000 short of realism. He yielded and we began the project. I knew I didn't want to see an hour of Chinese dance. My idea was about this Chinese "ballet" group coming to the US and being introduced to American ballet, modern and Broadway dancing.

I started with ballet: Suki Shorer, teacher *prima* at the School of American Ballet; taught them Balanchine; Paul Taylor company teachers taught them Paul's modern and Graciela Daniele introduced them to Broadway.

I thought all the results were C-minus. The teachers were sparkling, the dances had variety, but the students were fizzless (made up word). I began to believe that this was not a great experience for them. They do what they have been trained to do and that's it. Every decision was a group decision—no individuality. And they were not socially agreeable; they had not been taught how to meet other cultures.

The program was called *On the Move: The Central Ballet of China* and it was broadcast on *Great Performances*. And, it won a Blue Ribbon Award from the 1987 American Film and Video Festival. In 1988, *On the Move* brought me a Director's Guild of America Award.

1988

$\mathcal{P}$eter Martins adapted Bournonville's *La Sylphide* and the Pennsylvania-Milwaukee Ballet, directed by Rickie Weiss, a former member of the NYCB, had scheduled it for performances at the Academy of Music in Philadelphia. Catherine Tatge had agreed to produce it and I was invited to direct. Taping was planned for two performances.

I reluctantly agreed. I didn't like these kinds of assignments, directing live performances—I have no control and no corrective possibilities. This was Emile's game, but I was now freelancing and the advice was "Don't refuse any offer—you need the money."

A live orchestra was supplying the music and that's always the beginning of trouble. Unless the music is pre-recorded, no two performances will share the same tempo; that makes the editing tricky. During the rehearsal more trouble appeared: the Sylph, the star, fell off pointe at an exposed spot.

Peter and Rickie who, I was about to learn, was courting the Sylph did not take it seriously since we were taping two performances. My antenna wiggled and when the spot was about to occur in the first performance, I widened the shot. She did it again. Having been a performer with always-lurking stage fright, I was wary. At the next and final performance I was embarrassingly wide—and she didn't disappoint. Later, I learned from the founding director of the company that she was an inconsistent performer. Girish worked his magic, but there was only so much he could do. When Peter and Rickie saw the shot and realized there was no other, they were deeply despondent. But it was broadcast and it didn't stop Rickie from marrying the Sylph later. At last report she is now fifty and still dancing.

1989: Stella Adler

American Masters asked me to make a biography of Stella Adler. They were celebrating the Group Theatre, a collective formed in 1931 as a group of colleagues who believed in a forceful, naturalistic, disciplined artistry; with the idea of actors as a pure ensemble. A young Katherine Hepburn was noticed at one performance and asked if she planned to become a member. Her reply: "Absolutely not. I am going to be a star."

Stella was the leading lady of the group. She didn't like her colleagues then and she didn't like them any more fifty years later; so she refused to be in it. She got a solo project and that's what I agreed to.

What Stella didn't want you to know, she buried as deep as I had buried Twyla's *Camera 3* show. Stella never permitted a biography or any biographical articles. I hired her niece, the family historian and she didn't know anymore than I did. Necessary facts could not be verified; so I was not able to make a biography; I made a profile.

Stella was soft and flirty—and vulnerable—and she had my attention and loyalty within thirty seconds; so I made a profile of a great actress and teacher from a distinguished Jewish theatrical family, which included biographical materials. We had several interviews and she was always straightforward and direct with her answers. In taping, I avoided questions I knew she wouldn't answer. She was like Agnes—she would tell you, in a beguiling manner, what she was willing for you to know. It was easy to see how men were enchanted by her.

I was privileged to attend and film her classes. They were brilliant. She was not a coach; she was a genuine teacher of dramatic values. "It's not in the words, the meaning is underneath the words," she would say. If the scene was off, she would stop the actors; but if it was working, she would talk as it was playing with short suggestions and corrections. I saw a class in Los Angeles with a number of film celebrity actors who came, but didn't stay. Stella had no respect for actors who just wanted to be movie stars and acted the words. Melanie Griffith was one who left.

Stella Adler and Merrill

Stella and I developed a deep rapport that permeated the entire process of the making of this piece. The filming and the editing went smoothly. When we invited Stella to see our work, she became transfixed and began a dialogue with the characters on the screen. She felt rapture and I felt pride that I could give her a present to treasure. Afterwards she sent me a letter:

> *I never really said to you, in the fullness of my throaty voice, that working with you was a great creative experience which brought a lot of joy to a great many people. The film was successful beyond belief. You prodded and prodded me until you got what you wanted on the television screen. People were enthusiastic and were made happy and understood that you had something you wanted to say and said it through another person. Your questions were your roundabout way of getting a human truth from somebody who responded to you with a lot of love.*
>
> *With great affection,*
>
> *Stella*

Another letter to join Lincoln's in my treasure box. As you might suspect, I have a way with famed ladies over eighty.

1990: I HAD TWO PROJECTS THIS YEAR WITH INDEPENDENT PRODUCERS

*T*he first, an independent, innovative, quite pushy producer, invited me to direct a project with Les Ballets de Monte-Carlo. The company had commissioned a ballet from a celebrated Russian choreographer (name forgotten). The artistic director, Jean Yves Esquirre, wanted it to have a more extensive international presentation.

I always ask, on independent ventures, "Is the money in place?" I was assured it was, but I didn't learn the details until my assistant, Glenn Berenbeim and I arrived in Monaco, a glamorous cosmopolitan city with luxury accommodations, especially gambling. Then, I learned that we would be taping in Monte-Carlo, but from some backroom deal, editing in Switzerland. That reinforced my opinion that independent producers don't understand the word enough: preparation, rehearsal and filming time; nor do they understand that you need proper equipment to do your job. They do understand money and how to get more for themselves. So be it. We were there; so let's get about our work.

Since the first performance of Serge Diaghilev's Ballets Russes in 1909, the Principality of Monaco became one of several un-official homes for the company, where it performed each year at the Opera de Monte-Carlo as well as in the most famous theaters and venues in Europe. After Diaghilev's death in 1929 the company was soon disbanded. Later, an attempt was made to revive it, but that didn't succeed.

In 1985, Princess Caroline recreated a new company in the Principality, a project initiated by her mother, Princess Grace de Monaco and became its President and, I suspect, principal supporter.

My job was to build a program around the Russian commission and the ballets in the company's repertory. Jean Yves and I did it and we began rehearsals. I was astonished when I saw the rehearsal hall—it was small and the ceiling seemed to be no higher than eight feet—and this was in the studio that Nijinsky jumped? The attitude of all was agreeable; so the rehearsals went without event. We moved on to filming in the Opera House. I didn't know the camera crew or their skills; so I asked very basic tasks from them. I first recorded the company ballets, then on to the commission. After the second day Jean Yves came to me and whispered, "I don't like this ballet." I did not ask him: "Why didn't you find that out before?" I said, "There's nothing I can do about what we've filmed; if you want the choreographer (who was there) to change something, we can accommodate that." Nothing was changed; so we finished. I felt a cloud of black smoke had drifted over the project.

The brightest moment was meeting Princess Caroline. I had a point of reference. As mentioned earlier, when I was in Philadelphia I met Grace Kelly sitting in her *High Noon* costume during a taping session I was directing. She was everything I wanted her to be. Caroline, too, made a splendid presentation. She was indeed her mother's daughter. The first things I noticed were the shoes; they had to be Chanel. I had never seen Chanel shoes or clothes before, up close. Caroline was warm, friendly, complimentary—everything I would want her to be.

On to Switzerland by car: southern France to Genoa, Italy; then north to an inactive editing facility in Switzerland. I suspect that's how the producer got the backroom deal. I don't want to remember the agony of editing: primitive equipment, inexperienced personnel, wasted time—I was grateful to Glenn for his efficient records. And I was also glad to get out of Switzerland—all those mountains.

The film was finished and I still have a copy that I never looked at. I, also, never heard what happened to its distribution. The producer died not long afterward and Jean Yves soon left the company, accompanying his favorite male principal dancer to his new job at the Boston Ballet. Jean Yves' latest sighting was as a teacher at the school of the San Francisco Ballet.

THE ROMANTIC ERA, LATER IN 1990

The second project: a producer of my acquaintance told me about a ballet project he was producing at the *Cervantes International Festival* in Guanajuato, Mexico. The title was *The Romantic Era*, which was set in the mid-nineteenth century. The participants would be four internationally known ballerinas—Alicia Alonso (Cuba), Carla Fracci (Italy), Eva Evdokimova (America), GhislaineThesmar (France), the dance coordinator: Anton Dolin, former partner of Alicia Markova and the narrator: Erik Bruhn. I was invited to direct. Once again Catherine Tatge would be my producer. I was thrilled, especially because I was able to take my three longtime cameramen from Nashville.

The program was to begin with a *defile* (a dance introduction) with music by Chopin; then each ballerina and her partner would perform a *pas de deux*. We were to find that Miss Alonso was blind for any practical purpose and if she moved from one side of the stage to the other, she would be carried by her partner. Following these performance excerpts was to be a conversation with the four ballerinas. When it happened, my most remembered remark was from Miss Fracci: "Oh, Miss Alonso, when I was a little girl, you were my very favorite ballerina." I noticed that they all were very guarded—with knives ready. Finally, *Pas de Quatre* for all four. During the rehearsal Miss Alonso ran around yelling at each dancer, "You're wrong, you're wrong." Of course, she was the one who was wrong. But, it was a beautiful program with great variety.

NOTE: *Pas de Quatre* is a *ballet divertissement* choreographed by Jules Perrot in 1845 and on the night it premiered in London it caused a sensation with the critics and the public alike. The reason for this was that it brought together, on one stage, the four greatest ballerinas of the time. The ballerinas were, in order of appearance, Lucile Grahn, Carlotta Grisi, Fanny Cerrito, and Marie Taglioni. The order of appearance was done by age, from youngest to oldest, to squelch further confrontations between them, as this is a *tour de force* of one-ups-manship and is performed in that spirit to this day.

Catherine arrived early to see that everything was ready for rehearsal when the rest of us arrived. She was met by a stage with the lights un-hung and a crew sitting at the side, chatting. She asked and they promised; she went to dinner. When she returned, nothing had been hung. She asked and they promised. It happened once more and then Catherine did a Catherinism: she began to hang the lights herself. That struck deep into the crew's Mexican machismo. Need I say, the lights were hung when we all got there? The rehearsal and the performance went without incident.

Transition from New York to Where and What?

By the late 1980s, I began to think the unthinkable: "It's time to leave New York and television." New York seemed more crowded and noisy and television was rapidly pushing deeper into pop culture, a region I had no desire to explore. Many contributed to the degradation of television, but my special targets are the growth of excessive commercialism and MTV's encouragements, "Leave your brain behind and just have FUN—but, do it FAST."

It was not always thus.

In 1952 Sylvester (Pat) Weaver, NBC Executive and father of Sigourney, introduced his proposal of "enlightenment through exposure". He announced that "We must expose all of our people to the thrilling rewards that come from an understanding of fine music, ballet, the literary classics, science, art—everything. To program for the intellectual alone, is easy and duplicates other media.

To make us all intellectuals—there is the challenge of television."

In the early 1950s the airwaves were brimming with cultural and performing arts programs. The explanation was: There aren't many television sets and those are owned by people who can afford them. Gradually, as the sets and audience increased and prices were reduced, arts and information programs were transferred to out-of-way time slots: Sunday mornings and afternoons (until football staked a claim to Sunday afternoon).

Jack Gould of the *New York Times* explained: "The economics of television are, of course, at the root of this cultural evil. The costs run so high that the advertiser feels he must pursue the mob. In other media, he may specialize or deliberately seek out one or more of the limitless groups that together compose the illusory 'mass.'" In 1961 FCC Commission Chairman, Newton Minow stunned a broadcasters convention by calling television a "vast wasteland". A flurry of activity followed, but not for long. Relief came with the 1967 Public Broadcasting Act; which established the Public Broadcasting System (PBS). With the considerable generosity of the Ford Foundation, the core of the programming was cultural.

NOTE: For a more detailed account of the period, check an excellently informative book by Brian Rose: *Television and the Performing Arts*.

If you choose to ask me about the fifteen years of my life and career from 1967 to the end of 1982, I would tell you that it was the most challenging, stimulating and fulfilling period of my life.

CAMERA 3 (SEVEN YEARS):
I inherited "a walk through the marketplace of ideas"; a tradition of exploring fascinating and compelling subjects. I could unleash my curiosities. It was truly my graduate school.
DANCE IN AMERICA (FIVE YEARS):
Concert dance had never been seen on a continuing schedule; now it was scheduled for two years, but only began to slow down after twenty years.

CBS CABLE (Two years):

A proposed sponsor-supported cultural channel. Critic, Les Brown, observed its cultural orientation was selected not only "because no one had yet claimed the turf," but also because it "fits with CBS's image of itself. Culture is class."

Mister Paley announced, "At last we did something right." He was right about the programs praised for their excellence, but he was wrong about the advertiser projection. The advertisers played the watching and waiting game and were slow to sign up. A different way of viewing was growing: instead of advertisers paying for it, the viewer would pay for it and have more choices. It would be called subscription television.

WHERE TO NEXT?

I had traveled in Europe, Asia, Australia, Africa and South American and I knew that, although they were wondrous and often exciting places to visit, I was not an expatriate. I wanted to live in North America and I considered each region carefully and listened to my gut: I loved Vancouver, Seattle and Portland, especially the Oregon coast entered from there (the natives are careful to keep it their secret). It reminded me of the ocean in southern Portugal. And then I learned about continuing rain, except for July and August. I would choose not to live with too much absence of sun.

On a planned trip to Los Angeles I decided to stop off and see Bernice Petit, an old New York friend who had relocated to Santa Fe, New Mexico. I had been there several times in summer for the Santa Fe Opera, but I knew nothing about the near-by city.

Bernice was an informed guide; she took me to many places and told me the history of the oldest capital city in America. I was impressed by the charm, the beauty of the setting and the apparent ease of living. As many first-time visitors do, I fell in love with Santa Fe. I decided to give it a chance: I would come three times a year, for a month each, to experience the seasons and those months would be January, May and October. My first month was January 1991. A friend, originally from Los Angeles, rented me his house in Pojoaque, half an hour north of Santa Fe. The day after I arrived I was snowbound; then I remembered that January was a miserable weather month world-wide. May and October of 1991, each in a different house, were without event. Different houses in different areas of the city would become my plan of action.

1992: *George Balanchine's The Nutcracker*

On 1992 my January and May visits were without event. Then, a surprise! The news from Hollywood was that an independent-producer, announced the filming of *George Balanchine's The Nutcracker*. Peter Martins would be the artistic producer and he announced, "I want it to be a movie and not *Dance in America*." I didn't know how to take that; so I let it fly by. Emile had been in Hollywood for ten years and had directed two movies that made two hundred million dollars each. If anybody was snotty about Emile to me, my response was, "And how many movies has Mike Nichols made that grossed $200,000,000? Huh?" Happily and wisely, Emile was hired as director and I was invited to join in the project and asked to choose my title. It seemed ironic, but I chose Coordinating Producer.

At the beginning, a crucial decision was needed: should the format be wide screen or television 4X3? The producers didn't have a clue what we were talking about; so they said, "Both!" Of course, that was impossible. At that time, audiences hadn't fully accepted wide screen and subtitles; so Emile shot it with television framing.

The adventure of filming was exciting. Both Emile and the dancers were showing the best of their skills and Emile always kept a tension-free studio. I had a desk at his right and below so that I could see and comment on the action. I also had time to roam with my video camera and I was able to record several reels of diverting and informative backstage activities.

When I saw the completed film, it was wide-screen, which included unwanted and unplanned set materials, camera cords etc. These were the producers who bragged about their experience in distributing art films: "After all, we released *Hamlet.*" *The Nutcracker* was beautifully made; the dancing was brilliant and it deserved a more respectful showing.

DECISION

On the ninth month of the third year of spending time in Santa Fe, I decided to relocate there. I began the adventure "in love" with Santa Fe. I ended "loving" Santa Fe. I liked the diversity, as I did in New York.

As "the City Different" in the "Land of Enchantment", Santa Fe boasts of being the oldest city in America (if disputed, the-next-to-the-oldest). In 2010 it plans to celebrate its 400th anniversary. It is a city of extraordinary beauty and abundant charm; a city of architectural simplicity: A builder can choose between the ancient adobe Pueblo Style or the Territorial Style which began in 1846 with the annexation of New Mexico into the United States. Territorial is used mostly for government and commercial buildings. Most homebuilders choose adobe Pueblo Style—and it's usually some shade of brown.

By the beginning of the 21st century the population increased to 65,000; with Anglos becoming the slight majority; it is still rapidly increasing, but won't be recorded until the next census. The city is edging southward, but the growth appears more developer-originated than a singular-vision. With the exception of the Spanish and Indian markets in the summer and the Fiesta in September, many of the natives have released the Plaza, the historic center of the city, to the tourists—an economic food bank.

The most troublesome for me are the native Hispanics; many of who wish that the Anglos would all **go home**. As a group, they are not always friendly to ideas different from their own: "I do it like my grand daddy and that's good enough for me." And, "Just what do you know about it? You just got off the bus," was the war cry of the newly elected Hispanic female mayor, as she snapped her tongue in the faces of any Anglo City Councilor.

I had found the tender belly; I had also found respect and love for the city of galleries (the number rivals New York), the international Santa Fe Opera, the Georgia O'Keeffe, the Museum of International Folk Art and other excellent museums and the multifarious musical events at the Lensic, Santa Fe's Performing Arts Center.

I was a believer in the old adage: "Never marry when you are *in love*; fall out of *in love*, find LOVE, then marry." In the words of the immortal Jeanne Moreau: "Passion and love don't go together."

Unfinished

$\mathcal{T}$wo projects were not completed by the time I relocated away from New York. The time between my months in Santa Fe allowed me to complete them. The first was originated by Suki Shorer and Merrill Ashley. The subject was Balanchine's technique. No two were more qualified to present that subject than the premier teacher of the School of American Ballet and the preeminent ballerina of The New York City Ballet.

I was not the first director. A pilot had been taped and they showed it to me—it was boring and, I thought, disrespectful of Balanchine. They asked me to direct. I agreed, but I had an idea about format changes. First, I reminded them that Balanchine often said, "It's not my technique; it's Petipa's—I just use it."

Early in 2009 Arlene Croce, former dance critic for *The New Yorker*, wrote, and, I quote: "Balanchine shared with Stravinsky a firm belief in the labor of art as perpetual renovation. Stravinsky liked to quote Goethe:

'Everything has been thought of before; the task is to think of it again.'"

To think of it again: this is the task of the choreographer. It means imaging a nonexistent past, re-summoning the energies of previous choreographers whose dances have decayed or disappeared from memory. Balanchine assigned himself to rethink Petipa, because Petipa represented the sum of theoretical knowledge up to the end of the nineteenth century. Petipa, too, was more than a choreographer; he was a tradition. One of Balanchine's great statements was: "You must go through tradition, absorb it, and become, in a way, a reincarnation of all the artistic periods that have come before you. We all live in the same time together; there is no future, there is no past."

When you look at his ballets, you can see that he has speeded it up and made the steps clearer and more precise. So we agreed to call it *Essays in the Balanchine Style.* I proposed that the format be as follows: Suki explains the subject—for example, arabesque, port de bras, transfer of weight, etc.; then Merrill demonstrates it, followed by a small group of dancers who show how Balanchine used it in ballets. The ladies had selected nine subjects. I suggested that, since we were not under the restrictions of broadcast time limits, we let each episode be as long as it needed to be. Soon, it became clear that each time would be around forty-five minutes. That would make the total time around seven hours. It worked until the subject was jumps. The ladies found an abundance of material; so we taped two additional episodes, making the total time eleven hours.

The taping schedule was determined by money. Each episode cost nearly $50,000; which, at that time, was cheap. The speed of our taping depended on the fund-raising skills of our chief supporter, Barbara Horgan, Balanchine's administrative right hand.

We finished in 1993-94, ten years after he died and almost ten years from our beginning. I loved those ladies and their professionalism. I am proud of my part in this series. I think it is a memorable tribute to a man and teacher we all loved.

Tennessee Williams: Orpheus of the American Stage

*T*he second, unfinished project was a film biography of Tennessee Williams, deposited in my lap along with a request to direct it for the series *American Masters*, which bought the broadcast rights for three years. I was unwilling. I knew the plays and had seen the first casts of *The Glass Menagerie*, *A Streetcar Named Desire* and *Cat on a Hot Tin Roof*. But the preponderance of the biography would be his life, which I thought of as untidy, full of sex, alcohol and pills. After time and deep thought, I reluctantly agreed, probably because of John Lahr. I had met John in London and got to know him and his work. Soon after, he relocated to New York and became drama critic for *The New Yorker*. He had written amply about Williams and was well informed and agreed to accept the writing assignment. That settled, the producer, Catherine Tatge and I could move our attention to fundraising. We agreed that the best and, perhaps only, possibility was the National Endowment for the Humanities. Catherine inquired and there was interest—as soon as we had acquired the rights from the estate. Then the Endowment would talk more specifically.

I inquired about Tennessee's executor and found it was a minor former actress, now Lady Saint Just—she had married a Lord, now deceased, and lived in England. I further learned that her reputation was that she was not a lady, a saint, or just. Since John had more information, I quizzed him and learned that neither of them had a liking for the other—in fact, it bordered on hostility. He further suggested that I not tell her he was writing. That stopped me and launched a black cloud over the possibility of getting the estate rights. I explained that to John; we parted and I was without a writer. Catherine saved the project by suggesting a family friend, Brook Haxton, a college professor of English. I talked with him and hired him. Throughout the making of *Tennessee Williams: Orpheus of the American Stage*, he was a contributing and supportive companion for me.

I thirsted for an interview with Gore Vidal who had been an intimate during Tennessee's glory days. Catherine called him and he said, "I think I have a bit more to say about the Bird"—an affectionate nickname applied by Vidal. But Gore lived in Italy and had no plans to come to New York. I knew I had to get Lady Saint Just's permission; so Catherine planned a trip for the two of us to go to England and Italy for permission and interviews.

I thought the Lady would be tougher; so we started in Italy. Gore lived in Rapallo, north of Rome. I discovered that the entrance to his home was cut from the side of a mountain. The path to the front door was a single-file, not-long, but not-short stone walkway. Gore greeted us and once inside, we passed the library, stacked like the New York Public Library and then a table filled with photos. I noticed a photo of Amelia Earhart and I asked Gore about it and he said, "My father was in love with her."

The interview was in an enormous living room looking out onto the sea. Gore was formal but forthcoming in sharing his experiences with the Bird. He surprised me when he said, "I don't think the plays will last as long as his short stories." The long interview ended, I thanked him and we left as his companion was preparing lunch for a dignitary in the adjoining dining room.

Another day, another crew and Catherine and I were in England on our way to Lady Saint Just, past Stonehenge to Salisbury. We arrived at her home, a castle, sadly in need of repair, but I suspected it was not out of carelessness but due to lack of money. The Lady was cordial and we were cheerful and responsive guests. We were invited to dinner and, of course, we accepted. I decided that charm would be my tactic. No business was discussed, but the wine encouraged amiability. Next day we went back to talk and the Lady asked, "What do you want from me?"

I had a list and I read it to her. She agreed and then I said, "And, I would like to interview you." She was delighted. Her interview was more intimate and candid about Tennessee's behavior and she said what nobody else would say; "He killed himself with alcohol and pills." Tennessee's death was reported as 'death from trying to remove a bottle cap with his teeth'. No further details. Was he drunk? Did he swallow the bottle cap? Did he suffocate? Did he choke on the cap of the bottle?

Two minor characters in Tennessee's life-play had responded and been recorded, but I had others to persuade, all the time remembering that his major actress, Geraldine Page, had died. I wanted Elia Kazan and the principals of *A Streetcar Named Desire*. Kazan announced that he had said everything he had to say about Williams. Karl Malden echoed that. Brando had written an introduction to Stella Adler's book and my gut told me, "Don't even try." Happily, Kim Hunter responded and she gave a literate and informative interview. And, she was gracious. I next wanted to contact Tennessee's peer playwright, Arthur Miller. I called his agent and told him what I was hoping. Nulla! I did that twice more to the same response; so I determined he didn't want to play. Fortunately, Edward Albee did. He was not of Tennessee and Arthur's generation, but he was an admirer of Williams. He talked about Williams' influence on him. He was forthcoming and he was a gentleman. I admired his plays and now I admired him.

I had one more want—a critical evaluation of Tennessee's presence in the American theater. I most admired Robert Brustein, a critic who had founded a theater company and situated it at Yale, then later moved it to Harvard. I knew Bob informally and periodically we would meet. I knew he didn't like Tennessee's plays, but I decided to ask him anyway. I told him I wanted a piece about the effect of the *The Glass Menagerie* on the American theater. He cheerfully agreed and wrote a brilliant piece, better than I had hoped for—and didn't send a bill.

Girish was his usual masterful self in taking my ideas and making them better. *Tennessee Williams: Orpheus of the American Stage* was completed and broadcast on *American Masters*, which owned the rights for ten years. In 2004 the rights reverted to Catherine Tatge and me. She raised the money and I made the program. Each part is helpless without the other.

My Friendship with Eric—with the Aid of Stephen

$\mathcal{A}$s I was preparing to leave for my first trial month in Santa Fe, an acquaintance, a young ballet dancer, called to tell me about a young dancer he had met when they both were students at the Pacific Northwest Ballet the past summer in Seattle. He further told me that he lived in Santa Fe and suggested I call him. "His name is Stephen and he's a promising dancer."

I arrived in Santa Fe on New Year's Day, 1991 and made my way to a rented house thirty minutes north of Santa Fe. The next morning, I found that I was snowbound. When I was able to get out, I called Stephen and introduced myself. He invited me to a ballet class he was taking with two friends. I accepted and joined them at the studio. The class was a dismal affair: the two friends I would give a grade of "F", the teacher a "D" and I couldn't decide about Stephen. He, certainly, had the physical requirements; but I would have to see more to determine a rating.

During the following years and months I was visiting and exploring Santa Fe, Stephen and I would talk on the telephone or meet briefly. We began to see more of each other after I settled here in October 1993. Stephen and a few of his friends would appear to drink or smoke whatever was available and take a dip in my hot tub.

One day I invited Stephen—"But not your friends"—to come to dinner. He arrived at 4:30 in the afternoon. I explained that I was still working and I asked him to come back at 6:30PM—the same night. He arrived at 7PM with another young man he introduced as Eric. I was furious and berated Stephen for being late and not phoning me that he was bringing another person. I made the point several times which embarrassed Eric who said, "I think I should leave." I soothed the troubled waters by shutting up and bringing forth good food, wine and ushering in sparkling conversation.

The more we talked, the more I learned about Eric: he was not only handsome, he was bright, charming, charismatic and likeable—those qualities also characterized my father and the closer I looked the more I could see Eric's likeness in manner to my father. I must also add that Eric was staggeringly sexy. I was bewitched.

For the next few days I thought about "bewitched". I deeply considered our ages—twenty-nine and seventy-two—would not make happy boyfriends. I thought dirty old men were pathetic and I didn't see myself as a sugar daddy. "**Forty-three years**! I was old enough to be his grandfather. After exposing reality, it was clear that bewitched had to go. I told myself, "You can do it, after all, you gave up smoking." Then I began to consider what I really wanted from Eric. I suspected that he had a capacity for friendship which is something not many people of his age have. Then, I knew that I most wanted his friendship.

For reasons that neither of us can now remember why and how long, we didn't see each other. I moved into another house and I had a new Scottie dog, Annie Laurie. One night Eric and I accidentally met at a club. I think he remembered me but didn't remember my name. I invited him to come to dinner. He did and we began learning about each other. I knew he was living with a boyfriend, but we saw each other regularly and gradually our relationship deepened.

On Friday night, 4 December, 1996, I was in bed when Eric called, asking if he could stay for the weekend. Of course, I said yes. He arrived and I learned that his schizophrenic boyfriend had not taken his medication and Eric was frightened by his violent behavior. That weekend became what became thirteen years on 4 December, 2009.

Now, the touchy part of the friendship with Eric. He is an exceedingly private person; I learned from a prior writing incident that I have no right to write or tell about the personal life of others; therefore, it is not my right or privilege to write anything about Eric's past or present except for my participation in it.

When Eric moved in, he was working for a moving company. He was a matchless worker and appreciated by the company and he learned much that would be invaluable to us. But later, his body did not agree with that kind and amount of labor. I asked what he wanted to do and he told me he always wanted to go to college. I thought that was a terrific idea. Santa Fe has an excellent Community College. I suggested he determine what subjects and courses interested him and enroll. I further suggested that the aim was not a degree but information that could lead to knowledge. I also told him my rule: if a class or teacher is boring, leave and enroll in something else that piques your curiosity. He enrolled in courses in world history and sociology. Both were successes with excellent teachers. And there was a bonus: the world history teacher truly engaged his interest, which was rewarded by our future travel. He also took classes in computer and the Internet and, I think, he became extraordinarily skillful. That was to my advantage, since he became my teacher. Without his instruction I would never have been able to write my *Memories and Confessions*. Oldsters like me are generally fearful of the computer and the Internet and, unless there is a Chinese boy or equivalent in the neighborhood, tend to avoid them, which leaves the oldster someplace near the middle of the twentieth century.

I must not ignore telling that, at certain times in our friendship, I have been disgruntled and jealous. I determined to take it to therapy. The first therapist did not help me, but the second one did. He was a young man, barely forty, who knew how to open my understanding so that I could see that it was my problem: I was being my mother and Eric was not as docile as I had been. Eric and I were not peers. We were distant generations apart. Eric had his own individuality, his own experiences, his own habits—as I did. But his were different and asked to be respected. Eric was doing his part, but I was not. I began to try to change (after all, I did give up smoking) and I persevere.

Santa Fe Travel

After moving to Santa Fe, there were no demanding projects; so trips could be scheduled at will. Bernice Petit invited me to join her on a floating tour of the Amazon from Menaus (where the tributaries join) to the river's mouth; then on to Bahia, Brazilia and Rio de Janeiro. I went. I was particularly uncomfortable when I heard about the crime rate in Rio. There was a store that I wanted to see and shop, but I was advised to call them first. I did and they sent a car for me to go and return to my hotel.

Travel with Eric

I saw an advertisement of a cruise-tour leaving from Istanbul. Neither Eric nor I had been there; I asked, he was interested, so we signed up. We flew to Istanbul three days early so we could see the famous sights: Topkapi Palace, home of the sultans; Haggia Sophia, the greatest church in Christendom for 1000 years; the Blue

Mosque with six minarets and blue interior tiles and the Grand Bazaar, the ultimate shopping center.

The cruise began through the Bosphorous to the Turkish Riviera and Cyprus. Then, on to the Greek Islands—Lesbos and Rodos— where Eric drove us on a scooter and I found myself cramped on the back seat. Next was Jerusalem and the Dead Sea in Israel where I discovered that I could indeed float. The problem was that I couldn't get up until Eric waded out and put me upright. We cruised to Athens and then took a plane to the USA. On the way home we determined that we would never take another cruise. It's not jolly being two of a cramped and confined 200; our fellow passengers were boring companions; they spoke only about their kids and their expensive homes and cars. The number of meal calls was obscene. It's disheartening to see waist lines expand as you watch. We determined that, in the future, driving was the only way to travel.

From that resolve I had an idea: to search for the roots of western civilization in multiple episodes during a three-year period. For that, I chose to plan the itinerary and enlisted the driving skills of Eric and a superior travel agent.

Year 1—Italy:

Driving from Milan to a stop in Lake Como; then through Romeo and Juliet's Verona and Giotto's Padua to a lengthy stop in Venice; on to Florence and its treasures for a week, interrupted by a rail trip to and from Bologna (touted as the food capital of Italy) for lunch; then more Florence before driving again; this time through San Gemingnano (the towers) and Siena (the cathedral). Unfortunately the cathedral was wrapped; the exterior was being cleaned. (The Italians usually do their spring house cleaning during the tourist season). Then, on to Rome (past a group of aggressive African hookers along the road who scurried when Eric tried to take their picture) for a week of "this is why we came to Rome" (Saint Peters was also wrapped and being cleaned); then to Pompei (for exploration) and Positano (for relaxation) and back to Rome for the Vatican and the magical Sistine Chapel and a lively Italian finale.

Year 2—Egypt:
(*It was my third trip to Egypt; "Although you follow the same path, each trip feels fresh and different."*)

We began in Cairo and the, deservedly famed, Egyptian Museum and the pyramids; a flight to Luxor and the Valley of the Kings; an overnight sail to Abu Simbel and a flight back to Cairo. Touring by car is discouraged by the Egyptian government, pointing out the hazards. It is justifiably proud of the tours it arranges. Our tour (the sole exception to the rule) was notable for an extraordinarily informed guide and a small group of six including the Italian ambassador to the USA and his lady.

Year 3—Greece:

The plan was to begin in Thessaloniki, the capital of Macedonia and the heart of Alexander the Great's homeland. Two weeks before departure the Allies invaded Kosovo. I consulted the US State Department; it did not forbid, but it did advise caution.

The trip began: Albuquerque to Atlanta. The plane was late. So we travelers were re-routed to Brussels, Vienna, Munich and finally, Thessaloniki; where we were informed that our baggage was still in Atlanta.

Thessaloniki was knee deep in signs pushing the F word and insisting the Allies and especially the Americans, GO HOME! By wearing sandals (Europeans can always detect Americans by their footwear) and speaking softly, if at all, we were not identified.

After seeing Alexander the Great's birthplace (now, an empty plot of ground) and the ornate tomb of Philip, his father, we headed south through Thessaly and central Greece: Mount Olympus and the monasteries in the clouds of Meteora and Apollo's Delphi; then across the Gulf of Corinth to the Peloponnese and Olympia where Eric ran the track of the first Olympics (a videotape can prove it); then south, passing through Kalamata, (where the olives come from), to the tip of the Peloponnese where we stayed in a bed and breakfast converted from a medieval tower.

Next day we explored the Pirgos Dirou Caves which were spooky and scary; then north through Sparta (no visual memory exists of its glory days), the theater of Epidauros (the acoustics are as superb as publicized—it's entertaining to watch shy tourists take center stage to recite poems and sing songs they learned in the fifth grade) and Ancient Corinth; once again crossing the Gulf of Corinth to Piraeus to catch the dawn ferry to Mykonos for sun and reflection.

Three days later: a ferry to the incomparable Santorini for three days of astonishment; because the ferry didn't run every day to Crete and, because we were on an unrelenting schedule, we took a plane back to Athens and then forward to Crete. After exploring the ruins of the Palace at Knossos we drove east to the Venetian city of Hania on the north coast; then far west to Ayios Niklaos on the Mirabello Gulf.

I reflected on my plan to relocate to Crete: in addition to distance and language, giant resorts have encroached upon miles and miles of stunning white sand beaches. They appeal to European tourists, especially Germans, who arrive with the kids, granny, nanny and the dogs. They are loud and always first in line at the dining room.

We were tired travelers as we returned to Albuquerque by way of Athens, JFK and Cincinnati.

DIFFERENCES

In addition to the disparity of our ages and generations, Eric and I each had a different experience of reality. In growing up, I had been sheltered and taken care of by family, army instructors, and college guidance counselors. After I began a career in television and lived in rented apartments, I had a staff and a landlord; my cares were taken care of and I knew how to do none of them. I felt confident of my skills in my chosen profession; so I could be truthful and trusting. That was my reality until I met Eric.

Eric was raised by a loving and caring mother, in a relationship that remains so, today. His maturing was in a large urban, more hostile environment where his reality was totally different from what I knew. He experienced and he learned when truth and trust are merited. He also learned how to do those things that you learn when you don't have a staff or landlord. And he's been most generous in sharing with me, especially in my aging years.

It isn't always easy to find a television program or a movie that both of us want to watch; but our friendship is about learning from each other and sharing unconditional love and trust. Besides, I would never have learned enough about the computer to write my *Memories and Confessions* without him.

Eric's thoughts: "Friendship is a partial sharing of minds. The extent of that sharing depends on the depth to which the friendship goes. Each of a pair of friends constructs a mental model of the other in his or her mind. This model has both intellectual and emotional elements. The process of building and maintaining this model requires an openness of communication in which each friend provides the other with a progressive revelation—an honest inner exposure—of him or herself."

One of my favorite columnists, David Brooks, wrote: "Friends share a mutual ability to take each other seriously."

Arrival in Santa Fe

*M*y Arrival in Santa Fe was the first time in my life that I had been without a schedule; no obligations, except to pay the rent, etc.

I also learned that Santa Fe was gay-friendly and the only city I knew where gays and lesbians worked together; usually they treat each other as untouchables. I was impressed and joined several committees for fund raising and general promotion; it seemed I had no protection against persuasions to join. Then there were the pleas to give money; I became a victim of causes. I joined, participated and one day I was reminded of a comment of my father: "You are peeing in all directions and making a puddle in none." That stopped me. I took that to the thinking room.

I thought an appreciable amount of time, considering all of my activities and the demands of each. I decided that I would downsize my activities and chose to invest my time and concentration in three: the National

Dance Institute of New Mexico, The Lensic Performing Arts Center and Maria Benitez.

I met Maria Benitez when she joined the Dance Panel of the National Endowment for the Arts. With her, she brought celebrity as an exceptional flamenco dancer, which I later experienced. Maria became one of the few artists who could make me cry. She lives in Santa Fe and performed there in the summer. She asked me to join her board and I agreed. Later I would produce and tour with her second company to acquaint New Mexican Hispanics with their Spanish heritage.

The National Dance Institute of New Mexico

Before I left New York, Suki Schorer, master teacher at the School of American Ballet (SAB) and co-creator of *Essays in the Balanchine Style*, suggested I look up Catherine Oppenheimer, a former member of the New York City Ballet, who now lives in Santa Fe. After I was settled, I called her and found that her office was in her bedroom in nearby Tesuque. I learned that she had apprenticed with Jacques d'Amboise, the founder of the National Dance Institute (NDI) and that Catherine had the New Mexico franchise for NDI. We met and became instant friends; after all we both learned from the same master. Catherine was teaching at various places in Santa Fe and was eager to establish a home base, which she eventually did at the Pink Church, an arts space, which included a studio and office space.

I had worked with Jacques and had seen NDI performances in New York and was not impressed by the material nor the performances. I told Catherine this and was intrigued when she told me, "I have re-arranged the priorities." For Jacques it was the acclaim for himself, which often included his yelling at the dancers. For Catherine, there was no yelling; the quality education became the first priority.

Soon enough the Pink Church was too small for the growth of NDI-New Mexico (NDI-NM). I don't know how Catherine did it, although I surmised it was the deep pockets of the board she recruited, but she raised seven and a half million dollars, half for construction and half for endowment—of course, reality always overrides plans and the construction tipped the balance its way. The result was The Dance Barns—multiple studios and a performance space (combining two studios, this space holds an audience of 500 with 500 performers on stage), as well as administrative space and storage. A Triumph! The Barns were an immediate success—with much biting comment from other dance studios in Santa Fe. I must add that NDI-NM accommodates young dancers from less economically fortunate families and that means a lot of fund raising, but Catherine has remained faithful to her original priorities.

Physical education has disappeared in public schools and NDI-NM has given young people the possibility of moving their body parts—and they love it. Another part of the training reminds me of a story about Stokowski, the legendary conductor of the Philadelphia Orchestra and his rehearsals. He would arrive, give the downbeat, the orchestra would play and he would give all of his corrections over the playing. That is essentially the plan at NDI: to explain and let them do it, corrections over the doing, but don't interrupt or stop their energy flow. And the kids love it.

Recently, the School for the Performing Arts was added as an adjunct. I'm not familiar with their work other than with tiny tots. The regular NDI training begins with the 4th grade. At age twelve the dance curriculum begins: classes in ballet, modern, tap, jazz and musical theater. In the beginning, the dancers were graduated at fifteen. I strongly disagreed: "You should keep the program until they graduate from high school." The next year Catherine began the *Excel* program to do that. The first ballet group of thirteen was six girls and seven boys. I am most interested in the advanced ballet program and frequently go to the *Excel* classes. It was unexpected that the boys were better than the girls. This past summer, a talented seventeen-year-old male was accepted for training at SAB in New York. For me, that is the highest recognition. For the summer of 2009, two boys were chosen for scholarships: for one, a sixteen-year-old boy, his acceptance included tuition, lodging and transportation.

A year ago, I was attending an *Excel* ballet class and noticed the young male that I had been watching since he was nine. This day I was especially aware of his excellence. I thought, "He's doing what he's never seen anybody else do." I, at that moment, decided to give the dance portion of my extensive video library to NDI-NM (I've been taping since videotape arrived, which I think was 1968—or was it 1967?). Catherine raised the money (almost $100,000), Eric copied the tapes and Jesse (a young dancer) copied them into a giant computer brain. The result: *The Merrill Brockway Video Library*. I think it includes 120+ different programs of all dance genres. Now we are introducing dancers, beginning with the twelve-year-olds, to the library: how to learn what's in it and how to use it. If they can Google, they can use the library. And this generation can Google.

Again, I remembered Balanchine telling me, "Dancing is not the steps; dancing is in between the steps." I had seen how difficult it is for a young dancer to find the in between. To some it comes naturally, to others they continue doing steps. Nancy Reynolds, a former NYCB dancer started a video project called *Interpreter's Archive* in which Balanchine's original dancer coaches a company dancer in a role that he or she danced. I arranged for those tapes to become part of the video library. The first one I chose for them to see was Maria Tallchief coaching two NYCB principals, Wendy Whelan and Damien Woetzel in the final *pas de deux* from *The Nutcracker*. It was a revelation. The second tape was of Todd Bolender coaching Albert Evans, NYCB Principal in his solo from the third movement of *The Four Temperaments*. Albert performed, then Todd gave him an appraisal, "It was beautifully danced, but your performance was on the surface and theatrical; which is not the way I did it. I started from the inside and it grew outward—grew more intimate." I noticed that Todd didn't say, "Mine is the only (or the best) way to do it." Maria's coaching intimated, "This is the only way." From these two sessions I learned that Balanchine's instinct was to choose a dancer for a role; then he quietly coached as the role was developing. There was no "One Size Fits All".

I am so thrilled by the training that these young dancers' brains and bodies have absorbed that it doesn't matter whether they continue as dancers or not. With the training, they have the resources to better meet life's challenges. And this generation can certainly use such resources.

The NDI-NM Mission Statement is: "Teaching Children

Excellence. The core values to be learned are: work hard, never give up, do your personal best." This is what over 6,000 students are learning in New Mexico. That's because of NDI-NM's outreach program throughout the state.

THE LENSIC, SANTA FE'S PERFORMING ARTS CENTER

The story of the Lensic began when I met Nancy Zeckendorf, who was still fund-raising for the Santa Fe Opera, although her career had been as a dancer with the master ballet choreographer, Antony Tudor. In those days, Tudor and Balanchine were gossiped about as rivals. I know that Balanchine didn't think that. Their styles were different and personal. The fella who is suspicious of diversity always thinks that the fella who's different from his idol—in any way—is a rival and, even an enemy. Nancy and I soon worked that out and we became loyalists of ballet.

Beginning in 2000, Nancy's husband, Bill Zeckendorf, a famed builder in New York before they retired to Santa Fe, had an idea: to turn a 1931 movie palace into The Lensic Performing Arts Center. He knew how to do it. With Nancy in charge of raising $10 million and Bill's know-how, it happened. Renovation was from the street to the stage; from the stage to the rear wall of the building became state-of-the-art new construction. An advisory committee was formed and all the performing arts groups in the city each had a representative. I was the rep for Maria Benitez' Institute for Spanish Arts.

Participating was an education for me. I became familiar with each of the groups and began to see where each one's envy was directed and how each group kept secrets, including funder lists. When the building was completed and ready to begin operations, I was delighted to see how many barriers were broken down. The final triumph was a community box-office and each of the groups was a participant in it.

The next priority was the selection of a managing director. Nancy asked me to be on the search committee she was chairing and I accepted. As candidates were interviewed, my advice to Nancy always was, "If you don't think you can get along with him or her, forget it." It was no secret that Nancy would be in charge of running the operation. A local man who had founded a Shakespeare theatre was hired. At the same time I received a recommendation from Sue Weil in Los Angeles. That was my introduction to Bob Martin. I asked for a resume and learned that he had managed a theater in San Francisco. It was now my opinion that this job needed to be filled by someone who had done it; it was not a, learn on the job position. I presented the resume to Nancy who reminded me that a director had already been hired. I suggested we not reject Bob, but put his resume on the back burner. Coincidentally, it was becoming clear to Nancy and Bill that the hired one was not the right fit. Bob was called in, interviewed and signed.

The opening of The Lensic Performing Arts Center was the dominating event of the spring of 2001. Its first function was to serve the eight principal performing arts organizations; but the management was clever and, additionally, prepared a community-national-international brew.

As I write this, I've lived here nearly sixteen years. In the beginning when projects such as the Lensic would be proposed, members of the City Council would howl, "That's only for the elite." Happily, Bob Martin programmed the Lensic for all of the various interests of the citizens of Santa Fe and they attended their choices of the variety of events offered. Also, I experienced a change in the professional complexion of the city, which had been sub-level. Many who were skilled and experienced elsewhere, left their jobs and migrated to take high-level arts jobs here. For various reasons, they quit, but they didn't want to leave the city; so they stayed and became consultants and established their own businesses. They have given the city a cadre of professionals.

The Aspen Ballet began scheduling performances in Santa Fe. They were well received and I went to see their *Nutcracker*; which I found shockingly derived from Balanchine. I asked the two directors, who came of age with the Joffrey Ballet, about my concern; both said they'd never seen Balanchine's *Nutcracker*; then I asked them if they would let me send a tape of their performance to the Balanchine Trust for evaluation. They refused. Soon after, they became the Aspen Santa Fe Ballet. Then I saw a performance of Balanchine's *Apollo* performed by Aspen Santa Fe. That accomplished the impossible—it made Balanchine boring. I saw another performance of pieces that Arlene Croce, former dance critic of *The New Yorker*, would have reviewed as "Euro trash". I went to the boys again and said, "Let's get real. You're not a ballet company; why don't you call yourself what you are, a contemporary dance company?" I told them that the Santa Fe audience, unless they came from New York, Seattle, San Francisco or Houston, didn't know about concert dance, especially ballet and "You're selling them a false product. You're not a ballet company." No sale!

That stimulated an idea. With the support of Nancy and Bob Martin and the financial encouragement of Louisa Sarofim—whom I knew as a friend of the New York City Ballet and who lives in Houston but has a second home in Santa Fe—I proposed to present a yearly performance of a major ballet company. I couldn't afford full companies, but selected dancers and carefully chosen ballets could show Santa Fe what real ballet looks like. A few start-up questions needed to be answered including ticket prices and number of performances. A consideration was the size of the house, with only 800+ seats. I noted that expensive productions have a top price of $70.00 and sometimes $80.00. Bob and I considered it and agreed on a top of $55.00. That turned out to the right price for Santa Fe.

Our thinking was that we should present three performances: Friday and Saturday nights and a Sunday matinee. We also considered asking each company for two programs, but soon determined that policy didn't increase ticket sales. We also considered marketing. We didn't totally rely on the traditional print and direct mail, but added the Internet and radio; where I appeared on appropriate programs.

I began to consider the companies we would invite. I knew that I wanted the New York City Ballet to be the first, with a program to introduce Balanchine and Robbins.

I had worked with Sean Lavery, a former dancer and now Peter Martins assistant. He agreed to form a group of the best dancers. He did and they danced superbly: Balanchine's *Allegro Brilliante*, *Tchaikovsky Pas de Deux* and *Who Cares* and one of Robbins' piano ballets, *In the Night*. A healthy audience came, not a full house, but enough to tell me there was interest. I learned to love Santa Feans—they listened attentively and told you what they thought with their hands. Sadly, we had a financial hole. Happily Louisa filled that hole.

The next year I received a tip from a San Francisco Ballet friend. A former dancer, Jim now works as the director of the company school. He informed me that Yuri, a Russian-born and trained principal dancer with the company had organized a group of dancers and made a short tour of Russia. I invited Yuri to bring his group to Santa Fe and he accepted. They had a wide repertory; so we could offer two programs. The dancers were all principals and the performances were superb. They also did ballets from mid-19th century (*Giselle*) to contemporary (William Forsythe); that gave me an idea and a purpose: I wanted to present to the Santa Fe audience a variety of quality ballet, to show that ballet was not just one thing. Another pleasant surprise—the group had very loyal boosters who funded any deficit we had.

The next year, I read that Suzanne Farrell had formed her own company and planned to tour the east. In conversation with Margaret Selby, an old friend I had known at *Dance in America* and who, now, had her own division at Columbia Artists Management, told me she was booking the tour. Need I say I scheduled Suzanne's group?

Suzanne and her dancers arrived. I had worked with her during my projects with Balanchine and later, after her rift with Balanchine, with Bejart and again after she returned to NYC. We had been cordial but never close. Happily, I was able to take her to dinner so that we could unravel our past. I left with a deep respect for her willingness to talk openly about herself and her plans. We had scheduled two performances, preceded by a conversation between Suzanne and me the night before the opening. Each performance was with it's own selection of Balanchine ballets and each performance was a jewel. Suzanne has a Balanchine trait that I deeply admire: she doesn't want the dancer to imitate her performance; rather, she seeks and finds the individuality of the dancer to interpret the role.

I was especially thrilled by the second performance, which included *Apollo*. I have seen many interpretations, the last being from the Aspen Santa Fe Ballet, when they were trying to be a ballet company. I have also seen major principals of the NYCB perform this work. Each one had his way with it and each interpretation was interesting. But this was with Peter Boal. The character of Apollo is difficult—it begins when he is a youth and ends when he has attained Godhood and he and his three Muses climb to Olympus. Peter was the only one, that I've seen, who got the youth part.

I had not worked with Peter during *Dance in America*, because he did not join the company until after Balanchine's death, but I was aware of his blossoming career that began when he played the young prince in *The Nutcracker*. Although we knew about each other, we formally met when he accepted Suki's invitation to participate on *Essays in the Balanchine Style*. I could then see the artistry up close and I was mightily impressed. When he began an adjunct company, I attended performances to see his programming. I always liked the dancers chosen, but I sometimes had a different opinion about the choreography, but I much agreed with his aim to broaden the repertory to include more recent ballets by talented choreographers. I would share my opinions and always listened to him with interest.

I invited Peter and his adjunct company to be a part of the Lensic season. He accepted, but shortly it was announced that he had been appointed the new Artistic Director of the Pacific Northwest Ballet (PNB) in Seattle; which had been founded decades ago by Francia Russell and her husband, Kent Stowell, both former dancers with Balanchine. When I called Francia to congratulate her for hiring Peter, she said, "There was no other."

His first year, Peter was learning his new job and wasn't able to bring his company. Arrangements were complicated by the extravagant success Peter was having with his fresh programming and the response of his audiences, the press and funders. Eventually, he brought a group of PNB dancers and Peter's former NYCB partner, Wendy Whelan and they presented a program of Balanchine's *Tchaikovsky Pas de deux*, Robbins' *In the Night* and ballets by William Forsythe and Ulysses Dove. The audience was the largest of our series. I asked Bob Martin how he read it and he said, "It appears, ballet is catching on in Santa Fe."

NOTE: these performances were Peter's last as a dancer and he dedicated them to the Santa Fe audience and me.

Due to continuing success in Seattle, Peter and his dancers did not appear here for several years, but in 2008 I was able to announce that Peter would bring PNB to the Lensic early in October. I was especially proud of the program: Robbins' *In the Night* (our plan was *On the Town*, but the budget was prohibitive). Although it had been performed here several times, it always pleased the audience, (as Nancy said, "They don't remember"). Also on the program, Balanchine's *Jewels*: selections from *Emeralds* and the duets from *Rubies* and *Diamonds* and Balanchine's *Agon*, which deserves a comment. Often, when I get videos of young choreographers' work and they include 'trying to expand the boundaries of ballet', I see the video and say "*au contraire, Mon Cher*, you've just obliterated the boundaries of ballet."

In 1957 Balanchine premiered a new ballet with music by Stravinsky. It was as if he said, "If you want to expand the boundaries of ballet, I'll show you how to do it." He called the ballet *Agon*. According to Balanchine: "*Agon* is, for me, the quintessential contemporary ballet. Stravinsky composed it especially for us. In my opinion, it is his—and it is our—most perfect work; representing total collaboration between musician and choreographer. It is a new piece of diabolical craftsmanship; sounds like this have not been heard before. Musically, it is complicated; you have to analyze in advance what the music is about and what kind of sound it is and what it represents. Somebody has to analyze it; in this case, I did."

I am happy to announce that when the first night audience at the Lensic saw and heard *Agon*, they stood up and cheered.

Onward and upward with the arts in Santa Fe. In 2009 Peter has added Robbins' *Dances at a Gathering* to his repertory. I hoped to present it to our audience, but I think the current economy will not support that goal.

MISCELLANY

*W*hen I was in television and building a career, my life seemed to unfold in sequence, one thing followed another and a narrative was easy. When I came to Santa Fe, that all changed; there is no discernible sequence, except for my getting older. There are subjects that I dipped my toe in or explored and participated in. Also, in writing my memories, I have reconnected to my past and many memories and thoughts have wafted in, so I must take a different way to tell my story.

I understand miscellany to be a collection of different items, a mixture. And that is what the following is, a collection of subjects.

HOUSES

Bernice Petit arranged my first house. She had a friend, a former executive of Gumps in San Francisco, who retired to Santa Fe, bought a lot and commissioned the building of a house. It had three bedrooms, three baths. She soon decided that it was more house than she needed, so, since the lot was large enough, she had the builder build a smaller house in front. I agreed to rent the original house, sight unseen (you can begin to sense my naivety). This owner brought her executive San Francisco attitudes to Santa Fe, but agreed to an initial rent of $1500 a month. I wanted a lease and she reluctantly agreed as long as the rent increased every year (I was used to the New York rent increase every two years). I took two years, which sailed by uneventfully with a second year increase. Time for a new negotiation and she announced that her friends told her that the house was worth $2000 a month. I was furious and told her so and stomped out with "You can tell your friends that they ›››››››› " You can fill in the darts.

As I stormed out, the builder was outside making repairs. He asked, "How do you like my house?" I answered, "I like your house, I just don't like the rent." His reply, "Then why don't you come see the new house I'm building?" It was in a cul de sac, which I loved and the short story is I liked it—all three bedrooms and baths—and I rented it and got a five year lease with a 4% increase each year. The five years were uneventful. I lived there happily, especially when Annie Laurie and then Eric joined me. When the five years were up, I recognized that he wanted me to move because he wanted to sell the house (it was the height of the housing boom) and I had paid him $100,000 in rent. There must be a Plan B?

From the day I arrived I was told to "Buy a house. Santa Feans buy." Each time I told them, "New Yorkers don't buy; they rent."

One Sunday Eric and I drove to Sam's Club. On the return we noticed an open house sign. Eric asked if I would like to see it and I said, "Why not?" We found it was in the middle of a cul de sac. Only two houses had been built in addition to the one we were looking at which was in Mediterranean style with colored tile roofs on the entryway and a second story balcony. This was surprising; for the prevailing styles in Santa Fe are *Pueblo* and *Territorial*. Inside was another surprise: an ample living room with a cathedral ceiling and an open loft on the second floor. It also shared a gas fireplace with the dining room. Next to the dining room was an open kitchen and that's when I fell in love: a large kitchen with an island and lots of cabinets. There was an additional smaller open room on the other side of the kitchen. All kitchen counters and floor were covered with travertine, as were all the floors downstairs, including a half bath and a closet. And then I asked and learned that price was $275,000, unheard of in expensive Santa Fe. That price could only buy a shack, especially near the Plaza. The reason: the city was moving south and this new, developing area hadn't caught on yet.

The yard in back was another surprise; it was large and expansive and behind that was a green belt, which meant no building can be erected there. Upstairs was another delight: two bedrooms sharing a full bath and a master suite, the size of the two-car garage below. A short passage, off of which is a large walk-in closet, leading to a giant bathroom—my first thought: "a Roman indulgence". Two sinks, a jetted tub, a separate shower and an enclosed commode.

I didn't sleep much that night. I loved that house, but I had never owned a house and didn't know how to arrange it. But Eric did; so the next morning I called my investment manager and asked if I could financially handle it. He said, "Of course you can," and before nightfall I owned it. Just in time because there was another eager buyer competing.

Later, I would ask the builder why it had not sold, "because it's Mediterranean style." Apparently prospective Santa Fe buyers didn't like exceptionally large windows and a house full of light.

Our first delight was to bring Annie Laurie. She immediately took off and inspected downstairs then upstairs. When she came down, her decision was "I could live here."

Eric, too, loved the house and moved everything by himself, with the exception of the piano, inside or on top of his SUV.

As I write, we have lived here nine years, during which I have learned much about being a house owner. Eric was much more informed than I and he has been my guide—when I would let him. As a director I had an 'I listen to advice, then I will make a decision' attitude. Some of my choices were bummers: the backyard is very large and I wanted an enclosure for the dog; so I hired the contractor of my last house to build a wall—which is *de rigueur* in Santa Fe—and fence. Later I again hired him to build a balcony on the guest room as an extra treat for guests because the view is so beautiful. The quality of the construction was not first-rate.

Another of my bummers was the landscaping: my friend Bernice said that she had nothing to do the first year and volunteered to do it. The arrangement was that I would pay her a modest fee and I would pay for the plants. A few years later I noticed that she was an over-planter and was not a designer. She told Eric that she "loved to spend other people's money." She did and it was mine. Later, she decided that was enough and departed. My friend became my one-time friend.

But I've also had some lucky associations. After five years we knew the house had to be re-stuccoed. I received a bid of $20,000 after an appraisal. I was impressed, but Eric reminded me that we never accept the first bid without research. Coincidentally, my next-door neighbor was having her house stuccoed. I was impressed with the work and she introduced us to her contractor. His price: $8,000. At the end he said, "If you ever need landscaping, my cousin Nate is great." I called Nate; he surveyed the land, gave me a fair price and did it. The first year he did the back, the second year the front. He was a real designer and he made the yards look like a New Mexican Versailles. Weekly/monthly maintenance has been a problem; when I asked him for a recommendation, he said, "You won't need it; just call me in the spring to get ready for summer and in the fall to face the winter." After two years that turned out to be true. Some days, I feel I'm getting somewhere.

And that exposes a problem in the immigration puzzle. At least in Santa Fe, Mexican workers perform fast and expertly with intelligent guidance from a countryman who pays proper wages and prices fairly. I do not favor illegal immigration, but I think that, nationally, the issue should be explored more than it has been—with more intelligence and less prejudice.

How the Picture Window came to be

The house I bought in 2000 was the third house to be built in the cul de sac. I have seen the surrounding area grow and the city grow away from downtown and the Plaza.

Above my living room is an ample loft, which I used as my office until Eric's work expanded. I then used the downstairs, designated dining room as my office, because we entertain infrequently and the smaller family area, off the kitchen, became the dining room. Later, because I found that I didn't need that much space, we restored the dining room to its designed function and I moved to the smaller family room.

While I was installing the necessities—large built-in bookshelves, my computer, video equipment, a television and two chairs and supporting furniture—I became aware of two double-hung windows facing south. I remembered that, when we first talked, Eric said, "You come to Santa Fe for the view." Well, I never had a view. My first rental had no views, the second allowed me to go upstairs and see the sunset from a balcony—until the next-door lot was sold and the buyer built a house that blocked the sunset. Now I had a view. And what a view. I can see the Sandia Mountains in Albuquerque, fifty miles away, plus everything that's in between. For my eighty-forth birthday I decided to give myself a present. Eric and I went to Lowe's and ordered a picture window, five-foot-square, and arranged to have it installed.

Then I had a view. At the bottom of the frame is the top part of my adobe wall; on the right is the side of an old piñon tree. We have three large old, old piñon trees, which we happily saved from the bark beetles a few years past. Panning up to middle ground: far in the distance are little moving objects, which are cars and trucks on the Interstate highway, coming from and going to Albuquerque. Then there was a medium size mountain peak; after that a smaller peak closer to Albuquerque and, then, the large mass of the Sandias. That was the lower half of the frame; above that and half the frame, is the sky, usually filled with clouds. New Yorkers don't look at the clouds; if they look up, they see skyscrapers. I continued to study the clouds and discovered something from deep within me that was now appearing, the Spiritual. I looked up the definition: 'relating to, or affecting the human spirit or soul as opposed to material or physical things'.

Now, I'm a confirmed cloud watcher. I look at their multitude of designs, how fast they move—usually east and how they are slowly transforming into new designs.

I recently read an interview with Martin Sheen: "If you have an awareness that your life is not full and that you are not yourself, that is the beginning of the journey toward spirituality. I don't have a clue what God is. I would never, ever tell anyone what to look for. The only thing I would say is: the journey to spirituality is the journey to your own humanity. The more human you are; I think, the more God-like you are. And that's the genius of God." That affected me deeply as I continue to watch the clouds and get closer to nature and the way it operates. There's logic. And, I'm becoming more aware that humans are not cooperating.

Dogs

I grew up in a small town in Indiana during the 1920's. I was a lonely only-child and each year I would ask Santa Claus to bring me a dog. When I was five he brought Pal, a beautiful collie that looked like Lassie, of television and movie fame decades later. Pal and I immediately became each other's best friend: we played, we explored, we talked—I guess I was the one who talked, but Pal listened intently. He also liked it when I hugged him, which I did often. Pal showed me who he was: what he liked, what he didn't like, what he liked to do and, especially, how much he liked me.

Sometimes Pal liked to wander off by himself to check things out. That was not unusual in this small town. All dogs did that but were warned to stay away from the highway. One morning, after Pal didn't come home, my mother told me that Pal wouldn't be coming home. He had been shot by a hunter, who claimed he was chasing sheep. At that time the shared belief was that if a dog tasted sheep's blood, he would continue to chase and kill. Killing the dog was the accepted solution.

"Let's look for another dog." was an idea I couldn't agree to, I was full of grieving for Pal, which continued as I entered school. Years later a perky little toy terrier, white with a large round black spot on his back, appeared. That was my mother's way of saying, that's enough grief. We unanimously named him Toy and the word that best described him was, adorable. We became friends and from Mister Personality I began to learn the differences in breeds of dogs: their characters and personalities, their likes, their habits, their learning capabilities.

The demands of school accelerated and Toy became my mother's dog. For 50+ years I was dog-less while I was finishing high school, serving in World War II, attending college, then graduate school, apprenticing for a career in television in Philadelphia, practicing a career in television in New York and retiring to Santa Fe.

Late in my time in New York my workload decelerated and memories of Pal and Toy returned. I realized how much I missed the friendship of a dog. But what breed of dog in the city? At that time Danny Stadler was living with me and we went to dog shows, talked to breeders and read books. I concluded that it would be a Scottie; they are small enough, can travel and are bright, with excellent learning capabilities. I knew I wanted a female to name Annie Laurie (through the courtesy of Bobby Burns, 'For I will lay me doon and dee for the love of Annie Laurie'). This friendship didn't happen in New York nor in my first rental in Santa Fe ("No Pets Allowed"). But it did happen in my second rental. I heard from a friend about a Scottie breeder in Tennessee and I called. She had a newborn female available and her name was Madonna. I said, "I'll take her, but tell her that her new name is Annie Laurie."

Annie arrived in Albuquerque on Delta airlines one night in October, 1995. A friend had volunteered to drive us home. On our journey to Santa Fe I held this tiny, frightened bundle of fluff and we bonded. Our life together was simple, total togetherness. We lived together, slept together, traveled together, trained together. I didn't like doggie school: the tasks were too easy for Annie and I couldn't stand the other dogs' owners; so I contacted a trainer who promised, "I'll train her and I'll also train you;" and she did.

Our rapport astonished and pleased me. I truly believed that she understood English because her responses were so on the mark. She loved the enclosed yard where she could explore and chase tiny lizards under her favorite crabapple tree. I suspected that she knew me and my ways, better than I did. Often at night when other people were visiting and I grew weary, I would excuse myself and start to bed. Even if she might not be ready, she would follow, see that I was comfortably in bed and then go back downstairs.

During her third year I suspected that Annie Laurie needed a companion other than me; so I called her breeder; she sent Macgregor who had been a sire now retired. Annie revealed herself as an alpha dog, a leader (a surprise to me), but Macgregor was her generation and a gentleman; so I called him Mister Macgregor and they turned out to be different but perfect companions with a congenial, if not passionate, relationship. He saw things her way.

Macgregor had a roaring appetite and his eating had to be carefully monitored. One day we came home and learned that he had discovered a slight opening of the pantry door; he had burrowed his way in, attacked the bag of pet treats and filled himself to overflow. We found him in agony. He slipped off to the back yard to be miserable until his stomach slowly emptied.

Several uneventful years passed; then Annie developed a body complaint that the local vet could not define. We took her to a specialist in Albuquerque who also was puzzled until he surgically searched. She had lymphoma, almost unheard of in Scotties and it was malignant. I could not let my dearest friend suffer, so I kissed her goodbye and went outside while Eric took her. He told me that she kept looking as I left. My deepest regret is that I was too cowardly to stay and hold her as she was put to sleep. Eric said that she died peacefully without pain and I pondered on why my beloved pet could experience death with no pain and my human friends couldn't. My friend Danny, now a doctor and head of a hospice, was visiting and said, "There are ways."

Mister Macgregor was alone. He had no companion. Once again I called my friend, the breeder. She responded with Maria who became Lady Maria when she joined the household. She was a surprise; she was a white Scottie, something I had never known that Scotties could be. She had been a dam, now retired. The new surroundings made her uncomfortable until a month-long trip to the California coast put her at ease. It was delightful to see her unfold, leave her fears behind and contribute her individual qualities to the household.

Magregor and Maria were not especially compatible; each had a different agenda. There was no hostility, but there also was no congeniality. I needed something to bring them together. Again, I called the breeder and she responded with Maximilian, an alpha dog who got the household humming. I soon shortened him to Max

Now the Orkin Experience:

When I bought this house, I contacted Orkin and arranged for their bi-monthly pesticide services. It seemed a proper thing to do for the uninvited creepy crawlies. A serviceman was assigned; he was personable and responsible. During 2005 he developed physical problems and became unavailable. Later, I suspected that he had fallen victim to the poison. On the eventful day in August his replacement appeared. I always had concern about the effect of the pesticides on the resident dogs. The former serviceman assured Eric that it would be safe and that he was especially careful. The new serviceman announced that, because of the very evident families of ants he would be using a new poison. Eric pointed out the two Scotties and spoke of my fears, especially since it was a new poison. He assured Eric that it would be safe for them.

That was Friday. On Saturday Maria became ill. We took her to the Vet who treated her. She appeared to recover. On the following Thursday afternoon she was lying in Eric's lap when her insides exploded: she drowned painfully in her own blood. It was a ghoulish experience for Eric to be holding a blood-soaked dog in a room covered with the dead dog's blood.

During the week Mister Macgregor had breathing problems, noticeable when he climbed the stairs. On Saturday morning the problems became acute; he had great difficulty in breathing. We took him to the vet who began oxygen control. He then recommended Macgregor be sent to the specialist in Albuquerque. I agreed. Soon after midnight the doctor called to tell me that Mister Macgregor had died. The thought that he, wondering what was happening and where were his friends, haunts me. He died alone and I didn't even get to hold him.

That is not the end of the dog saga. Max remained; so once again I called, now really my friend, the breeder who sent us Mini Pleasures, shortened by me to Minnie; so we now had Max and Minnie. I learned later that Max had been the father of Minnie's first two litters; so they recognized each other happily. I will let them get reacquainted while I tell you the follow up to Maria and Macgregor.

I decided to sue Orkin. Eric did an extensive Internet search and I presented it to my lawyer and asked, "Do I have a case?" After reading and thinking she said, "yes." She took over and it wasn't fast or easy. After a year of sparring, Orkin asked for mediation which was great for me, I didn't want to go into court with those expenses. Orkin sent three representatives and they first denied Orkin had anything to do with the death of the two animals. Eric had made enlarged photos of each dog, which I put in front of the reps and said, "This is what we are talking about." The Orkin three went to another room and the mediating began. Agreement didn't come easily: back and forth, until we understood that time was running out for them and they wanted to catch their planes. Their final offer: $19,500 "take it or leave it". We took it; it was an offer that astonished the law office: "Animals have never gotten that much financial recognition." My lawyer got her share, Eric got his share and I got my protesting citizen share.

At home with Max and Mini: both had been neutered; so there's no hanky panky, but there's a lot of togetherness. Max likes to sniff her parts and she likes to sleep with her butt touching his. They both sleep with me and each likes body contact with me, she the upper part and he the lower part. It's all warm and comforting for each of us.

By this time I have owned and lived with five Scottie dogs, which entitles me to an opinion. In characteristics and behavior, each has been different from the others. They all have only one thing in common: they all like to eat. My bargain with each, on the advice of the breeder, is to feed them at 7AM and 5PM; that includes a treat of two carrots after each meal. There may be a small snack mid-day. No table food. The breeder advises the nutritious bagged food we have flown in.

This has led me to think about wider implications. Is it possible that all creatures—human, animal (I don't know enough about different kinds of fish or trees to include them)—are different one from another?

Is it possible that the Earth's first peoples could not handle that idea of diversity; so they came up with ideas to deny it: clans, skin colors, where you come from etc. To see only that is to miss a gift. It's the truth that few want to know about.

Merrill with Max and Minnie

I grew up in a small town where everyone shared the same religious beliefs, the same political prejudices and the same rules for social behavior. It was all very bland and very boring. My next adventure, the US Army, was no introduction to diversity; it preferred, yea insisted, that each one saw it their way. It wasn't until I arrived at Columbia College in New York City that I met diversity. At first, it was bewildering to find different-ness and variety. I found that it was often difficult or annoying, but endure and rewards will surface. And that's why I chose to live in Santa Fe.

FRIENDS NEAR AND FAR

When I started this section, I discovered that I had *beaucoup* lists of friends based on location, time, memories, the period in my life, those still active and those who are active on the telephone with or without occasional but infrequent visits.

As I looked through the various lists, they reminded me of those Christmas greetings with an attached note from the sender that tells the names of all those friends seen and enjoyed during the year and the receiver doesn't know a single name. I concluded that lists are fine for donors and such, but they don't work for friends—someone is sure to have hurt feelings; I will not offer anything resembling a list of friends.

In the memories I have used first names, mostly, to protect their privacy and I have written about our relationship together, not any private details about that person. One thing they all share: Accomplishment. I think of each one who has become a friend as a unique individual. None of them belong on a list. They each know who they are and the quality of our friendship and I respect that.

RETIRING

The early days of my retirement were off-putting. The work discipline I had followed for decades was replaced with an overpowering emptiness. I soon realized that retiring was my choice and decision and that Santa Fe was a wondrous place to live. Further, it was my responsibility to fill the emptiness. I am empathetic to men my age who are reluctant and even resistant to retiring. They are averse to meeting the great unknown.

When I retired, a part of me I had never known began to appear. The "director" began to fade away and I became less goal-oriented and more observant and pliant. Later, a therapist told me that it usually takes about four years to adjust to retirement and she wasn't too far off in my case.

It's a wonderful feeling to find a new part of yourself that you never even knew existed. Retiring is about taking deep breaths, sitting back looking around and learning about yourself in ways you've never known or suspected—and enjoying the newness.

CANCER

Doctor Robeson, a Urologist, whom I infrequently visited, called to tell me the results of a recent test: "I think you have prostate cancer; when can you come in?" Of course, I made the earliest possible appointment. The next test confirmed it, but, happily, it hadn't metastasized. First, method of treatment: since I was past seventy, no surgery (which I didn't want, anyway); the radiation spray of seeds was new and Dr. Robeson didn't believe in using anything that hadn't been tested for ten years. Radiation seemed the best; so I was scheduled for five-days-a-week for eight weeks of treatment. Before we began Dr. Robeson gave me a choice: 1) to take a powerful shot that would suspend the function of testosterone, or 2) not to take it. I took it. The promise was that testosterone would return after the treatment.

The procedure of radiation was a new experience for me: it was not painful, but I didn't consider what it was doing to my insides. I continued my two large drinks of scotch and soda nightly. I didn't notice anything different in my behavior, but Eric did; I didn't listen until he took a photo of my lying on the kitchen floor, passed out with Annie Laurie looking and trying to determine what was going on.

The eight weeks ended, but it was some time before I learned the effect of the radiation. Good News: only a small tip of my prostate remained.

Not so Good News: after three months (the previously announced time) my testosterone function had not returned. I reported that to the doctor who said, "I can take care of that." I said, "Let me think."

Before me was one of those life decisions. I thought of my experiences with sex, which were not frequent nor especially joyous. I grew up at a time and a place that sex was connected to love; that was hard enough to find with the paucity of choices. Then the Roaring Sixties and promiscuity arrived. I was not comfortable with that. I finally concluded that sex had not enhanced my life (in my time nobody knew how to do it—it was like trying to play the piano with only "doing what comes naturally"); so I thanked the doctor and declined. That changed the fabric of my life.

Two other after-effects of the radiation: my plumbing was completely discombobulated, which meant it was "forget the planning; anything can happen anytime, anyplace." Also, I was in my third and, it turned out, my last semester of a Spanish course at the Community College. Nothing remembered. Short-term memory shot.

No cancer, but there was a price and I continue to pay.

PSYCHIATRY

Psychiatry has played a big and important place in my life—once I discovered its existence. My trouble began in my dorm room at Columbia when I didn't leave for three days. I knew something was wrong and needed to be fixed. I remembered a young man in the army who had war problems. He was now an instructor in the French Department. I went to see him and he introduced me to the idea of psychotherapy and suggested I go to a traditional German psychiatrist whose theory was: "I speak after you talk." I didn't talk because: I didn't know what to talk about. Our sessions were only one. Then I saw several suggested therapists, each with different approaches. Some were helpful—most were not.

My most memorable experience was with Albert Ellis. Dr. Ellis believed in short-term therapy that called on patients to focus on what was happening in their lives at the moment and to take immediate action to change their behavior. Neurosis, he said, was "just a high-class word for whining." He recognized that people are born with a talent for crooked things—distortion of perception that sabotages their innate desire for happiness. He also recognized that people also have the capacity to change themselves—to establish new ways of being and behaving.

Dr. Ellis was known as irreverent and charismatic; he was also called the Lenny Bruce of psychotherapy. I found our sessions fun—he always started a session by taking off his shoes and putting his orange-stockinged feet on a large footstool That was a signal that we were going to be informal. Our conversations were open and honest on my part and his comments were meaningful and helpful.

Later I learned that his streamlined, confrontational approach to psychotherapy made him one of the influential and provocative figures in modern psychology.

Then, in Santa Fe I had two therapists. The first was a lesbian from New York who had all the references. Eric joined me several times and his friend Bruno once. Later, I realized that I wanted her to explain to Eric that I was right in my thinking about and expectations of him. It didn't work. But the next therapist, a young gay man, clarified it: through him I realized I had become my own mother. I was jealous, possessive, controlling. It was my problem to solve and I learned how to solve it because of Albert Ellis and his teaching me how to solve it.

At the time I write this I have done well. Eric is his own person: he has his own habits, preferences, experiences and all the other differences that make human beings unique. I truly believe that and now I have to live it. Eric cares for me and he also cares _for_ me. I am blessed. I am also reminded of Albert Ellis and how he prepared me.

SMOKING AND DRINKING

Smoking:

Since they are separate and have different paths in my life, I'll begin with smoking. I started smoking at fifteen and my mother commented that, "I see you've added smoking to your many accomplishments." In my generation it was the thing to do; just as, at this time, girls of that age are getting pregnant and having babies. It's a wish for adulthood.

My smoking was practically non-existent until I became a part of television. I remember one time in New York when I saw a specialist for whatever reason and the first question he asked was, "Do you smoke?" I told him I did. He said, "not anymore. Give them to me—and the lighter." I did and I didn't smoke for two years. Then, one day I was standing in front of my boss' desk discussing a tense situation. I noticed a pack of cigarettes on his desk, reached for one and smoked it. Three cigarettes later and I was back on the habit. That accelerated to three packs a day. Why? Society permitted it, until the Surgeon General's judgment was circulated. I read, but I still continued smoking until one night in 1983. I was at a party with a British producer and I was smoking. He said, Merrill, "We don't do that anymore" For some mysterious reason that clicked with me?

I participated in all the stop-smoking programs available at the time; they were all countdowns to 0; I usually left around 3-2-1. I also tried hypnosis, which I passed with a 98% rating and smoked in the cab on the way home. And then I heard about a Chinese acupuncturist. What did I have to lose? Three times a puncture on the face-side of the ear and I have not smoked since. I asked him, "How? Why?" He told me that he had two nurses who wanted to lose weight. He punctured in the same place. They lost weight, but they also stopped smoking. Ergo.

Now it is twenty-six years later and I have an aversion to cigarettes and cigarette smoke. The only remnant of those years is a slight spot on my lungs which is X-rayed quarterly. After several years the spot remains unchanged.

Drinking:

Although my father was a heavy drinker, that had no effect on my life until I got to Columbia after the war. And, even then, my drinking was infrequent. Even during my television apprenticeship in Philadelphia, there was no time for drinking; I had so much to learn and practice to be a director. Early in my return to New York as a director I began to open up my social life—and drinking began, slowly. I never drank when I was directing. I was switching cameras live and my reflexes needed to be intact.

Gradually, almost imperceptibly, my drinking accelerated. I remember the times that my friend, Sue and I favored Bombay gin; I remember that I liked to have lunch dates at the Russian Tea Room, where I had two, often three, gin martinis. That was before vermouth had been introduced to vodka. I was wasted for the afternoon, but I didn't have to direct.

Finally, a voice inside me said, "that's enough." I looked at the remedial proposals available at that time, found them tepid; so I went to AA. I lived in New York so there were many meetings to go to at different times and I took advantage of several. I went to two or three a week and I never found one that was boring. Each and every life story was riveting. I couldn't challenge any one of them, so I just listened and gradually stopped drinking.

After a year of innumerable meetings and powerful life stories, I looked at myself and said, "You have become the world's most boring man." I stopped going to AA. Later my friend, Faubion, said, "I never understood why you went to AA. You're not an alcoholic, you're a drunk." And he was right.

Drunks are told by their doctors that moderation is not possible; that they should go to AA. That's what my former doctor told me. He was wrong. Today, after a year or so, I drink two scotch and sodas, made in the same glass with scotch to a measured level and not before 6PM. I sleep peacefully.

Unexpectedly, my Santa Fe doctor of fifteen years decided he would no longer accept insurance. I could understand that he wanted to simplify his life; but so did I. My peer friend, Susan, suggested I see a young doctor she had discovered, and who recently arrived in Santa Fe. I made an appointment and found him to be young, bright and with impressive training.

I began to think about the "sleeping peacefully" that I mentioned in a prior paragraph. In the past, I would go to bed, my mind would feed me ideas, memories, regrets and fantasies and I would remain sleepless. Then I remembered *Cat on a Hot Tin Roof* when Big Daddy asked Brick, "Why do you drink?"—the reply, "I'm waiting to hear the click." I understood that. My response was two large glasses of scotch and soda from 6PM to 10PM.

By Then I could go to bed and hear the click.

But I was kidding myself. Each morning I would wake up with a hangover and not especially ready to greet the day.

An Update from 2009

After presenting Peter Boal and Company in October 2008, I was exhausted and had a cold: one week of cold and one week of recovery. I noticed that during that period I hadn't drunk anything but ginger ale and I hadn't wanted to. I remember my friend, Jack Willis, telling me, "It didn't bother me to give up drinking, but I miss the habit." I determined that I didn't want to stop drinking forever; I occasionally wanted to have a drink of scotch without feeling mortally guilty or ashamed; so I substituted ginger ale for scotch at 6PM each night and I can have as many of them as I want and wake up fresh the next morning.

As I conclude this journal it's still working, because my doctor prescribed a nightly pill.

Innocent and Trusting

I was born into the Roaring Twenties; I began to be aware of the outside world as FDR took office. That was not easy because I lived in a small town of 800 people, each was innocent and trustworthy; nobody locked their doors at night. There was no murder, burglary or robbery, fraud, etc., although there was a rumor of embezzlement of the bank by a trusted employee.

The army was a protected environment. In New York I learned the rules for living in a large city and I was protected by the college, when I was there. That held for Philadelphia and my return to New York. Also, from the time I became a director I had a staff that knew of my gullibility and protected me from enticing con artists.

The trouble began with the Internet and e-mail. I became a mark for people who wanted me to give money for a scheme or a cause and then there were the "get rich quick" offers. It was then that Eric began counseling me. Eric had spent almost a decade of his twenties in Los Angeles and learned street wisdom. He was aware of the traps of contemporary society for the senior citizen. This was not easy for me to absorb, I was still innocent and trusting.

After I visited Santa Fe and wanted to know more, I accepted an offer to buy a time-share for $10,000, one bedroom, one bath, because I was still innocent and trusting. After I had moved, I bought another one for $2,500 (in hind-sight I haven't a clue to the reason). Years past: I never used them; no friends used them and each year I was billed for $700+, per year, for maintenance. At that point I decided to try to sell them and that began a trail of lies and various techniques of conning me. But I remained an optimist and a creature of believing. I estimate I gave $4000. Eric found out and offered advice, but I remained an optimist ("Someday, someone will..... "). Recently, I received by mail an announcement from a company, coming to Santa Fe, which stated that they wanted to acquire my timeshares. I called the number and made an appointment. I decided to go and asked Eric to come with me. The meeting was a revelation: The representative told me they were not wanting to buy but to acquire timeshares. Next he told me there was no venue to sell them, private or public; as long as I held the deeds I would be assessed the maintenance; but they could take them off my hands. I could lose the deeds for closing fees of $4000. Eric had been asking questions to which the representative did not respond in a cordial manner. Eric told him we always researched and talked before we made any decision. On the drive home we both agreed that we had been accosted by a used car salesman. I knew I didn't want to give away both timeshares and pay $4000 to lose the deeds. His sales pitch was designed for first-time sellers and old people who had illusions of thousands for their shares. They would be easier to persuade and would take the offer. I had been lied to and conned too many times. Next day Eric took to the computer for information. On the first site he found, "Don't hang out with those guys." Good advice; Eric continues to find who we should hang out with. Later I received a bill for the yearly maintenance fee. I paused, only momentarily, before I gave both shares to the home company. No profit but no more expense.

Slowly, my innocence and trusting are beginning to fade.

REFLECTIONS ON MY PAST RELIGIOUS ACTIVITY

With the exception of a short period of Episcopalian fervor and baptism—I think it was really about the theatricality—while I was at Columbia, my religious life was non-denominational Protestantism. My parents irregularly attended the Community Church. I remember, as an advancing piano student, being asked to play for services. I did, but not many. The young pastor, a graduate student at the University of Chicago and I liked each other and he asked me to visit him and his wife and see an opera. That made my head rush. I was already an opera buff and had many RCA Red Seal records of my favorites. "Which one? *Carmen, La Boheme, IL Trovatore?*" The reply, "None of those; we're going to see *Der Rosenkavalier* by Strauss." I had no idea what that was, but I went and I was transfixed. I was seeing a world I'd never known. The Marschallin was Lotte Lehman; I didn't know who she was, but I <u>heard</u> who the Marschallin was—and I remembered. That performance introduced me to adult musical life.

Since these experiences, my religious life has been non-participatory. My only thought-provoking experience was reading Tolstoy's searching out the actual words that Christ spoke, without commentary, *The Gospel in Brief.* I began to understand how Saint Paul had taken a journey to Damascus, had a vision and marketed the message. That was the beginning of trouble.

TRUTH

As a child growing up I was taught, "Always tell the truth." It didn't take me long to find out that, if I always told the truth, I wouldn't have any friends. So I put truth on the back shelf while I confronted the exigencies of living.

I didn't really think about truth again until I was at Columbia College and was introduced to the ideas of Socrates and Plato. I remember that Socrates dismissed all the Greek Gods and said, "There is only one God." For that, the Greeks rewarded him with a drink of hemlock. I remember that Plato said that truth was born in each of us, that it is each one's perception of reality and living and aging will give us more information about our truth.

"Isn't it a bad thing to be deceived about truth and a good thing to know what truth is? For I assume that by knowing the truth you mean knowing what things really are." I also understand that my truth is not anybody else's truth. Then why do religious organizations tell me "You'll burn in Hell," because my truth is not their truth?

THE PACIFIC

Beginning in 2000 Eric and I escaped the holiday Christmas and New Years hoopla of Santa Fe by taking the dogs and driving to San Diego and renting lodging on the Pacific. After experiencing each of the three beaches, we decided to move north to Oceanside where, in low season, we could rent a house on the ocean for a month at the same rental as a ten-day Christmas holiday in San Diego.

Eric and I are both Pisces; so, for both of us, the Pacific is like coming home. My greatest pleasure was walking on the beach for an hour each day. Then, three years later I began my walk; after ten minutes I had to sit down—my physical diminishing was underway. We continued to go and I began writing my *Memories and Confessions* there in the fall of 2007. A return in 2008 was prevented by my presenting Peter Boal's Pacific Northwest Ballet.

To own a house on the ocean would be the dream, but in 2007 that conversation would begin with three million. Now with the economy so low, it might be half of that. We jokingly say, "The first thing we'll do is buy a house on the Pacific—after we win the Lottery!"

AGING, THE PROCESS OF GROWING OLD

The fanfare to announce my aging was in Greece at the Temple of Delphi. The hill to the Temple was long, high and steep. After I had climbed a bit, I told Eric, "You go on; I'll wait for you here." I thought nothing about it; since, when I retired at seventy, I had the energy and endurance of a fifty-year-old; from then, until my early 80s, that is. Soon after entering my eighties I found that this was new territory, unrelated to my first eighty years. This would be a period of bewildering change and I determined that I would not deny that something was happening, nor would I become a grumpy old man bemoaning and railing against the loss of the past. Fortunately, my brain and longtime memory were operating, or I couldn't have written this account of my life. My body was something else:

The first to go was my balance; I could one day, I couldn't the next. I consulted a neurologist who assured me that the widely held belief that the trouble was in the middle ear was a myth and sent me for an examination of my cerebellum and a check of the efficiency of vitamin B12. I passed; then he sent me to physical therapy. I took a series of classes and learned that my foot muscles had not been exercised enough and had lost the ability to function properly. My thought: "How can I regain balance and walk again?" That thought remains with me today.

For starters, I have chronic bronchitis, discovered by a spot on my lungs. From X-rays every three months it has remained the same. I am sure that the reason was smoking from the age of fifteen to sixty.

A further discouragement was my doctor discovering that I was losing oxygen with exertion. He sent me to my second night at the sleep clinic. The first night, a few years before, revealed that I had sleep apnea, the second that I needed oxygen. The situation is aggravated by Santa Fe's altitude of 7,000 feet. Nighttime was easy, since I have a C pap machine for apnea and breathe though a mask. Oxygen was easily plugged into that. For exercise and any exertion I have a portable oxygen container.

Recently, I received a fortunate unexpectedness: a new and gifted Pulmonologist. After my second visit she advised a new Pulmonology rehabilitation clinic. I enrolled. The clinic was skillfully organized and operated. I learned that I had been breathing incorrectly all my life. The two-hour sessions were three days a week for eight weeks. I graduated with information and exercise routines.

I bought a treadmill and use it every day after a warm up I learned at the clinic. I use the treadmill daily at the advised slow speed, which strengthens leg muscles. After six months I began to feel the difference. I still can't walk long distances, but I can walk. And I've added balance exercises to my daily routine. I returned to my former fitness center to adjust my three-times-a-week routine with my new information. My two trainers are first-rate. Remember: "No complaining about what you can't do. Search out what you _can_ do." And do it!

Further, I devised a few questions for me to think about on my adventure.

Nutrition

"_Are you eating healthy foods? Examine what you eat: do you have exceptions that slowly become habits?_"

I'm blessed to have Eric who does the cooking and is a devotee of Dr. Andrew Weil, a wise man about food. No junk food! Eric started with: no processed food. That increased to: no food with growth hormones, antibiotics, or animal bi-products. He convinced me that no diet works; nothing is forbidden, everything in moderation. My liking for desserts and ice cream is now infrequent. Whole grains, fruits and vegetables; chicken and fish, brown rice have become the norm for me. I'm a creature of changing habits and I must admit that I feel better. We do have an occasional steak. (I spare you my diatribe on McDonalds and Burger King) I'm truly surprised how easy I have surrendered eating and drinking habits of my past; it must have been a secular epiphany. But I still miss peanut brittle.

Exercise

I ignored exercise during growing up, college and television in Philadelphia. In New York I realized that I was, then, in the Big Apple and that I should get about it. I didn't have a trainer then, but I did determine to exercise three times a week, even when I had to wait for a bus on Riverside Drive in a snowstorm early in the morning. Probably a lot of exertion was wasted, but I developed the habit. In Santa Fe I joined a fitness facility. There I had fitness advice from trainers three times a week.

Sleep

Recently, I read articles reflecting sleep surveys and learned that Americans are the most sleep-deprived country in the world and it deeply affects their health. I began to ask around and found that only my peer group gets a proper amount of sleep and that's because they are retired and go to bed early and wake up early. There are many excuses from other groups: work, homework, late night activities, television, among others. You can't watch Leno or Letterman or a late movie and get enough sleep for tomorrow's work or school. After the 10PM news and weather—and before sports—Max, Minnie and I head upstairs where they are asleep as soon as they settle on the bed. It takes me a bit longer, but all of us wake up by 7AM, ready for the day's surprises. Best of all, I don't have a hangover.

BAGGAGE

"Ask yourself to consider every idea, deep-seated belief, opinion, prejudice, certainty, etcetera, etcetera, that you've had since the beginning of your consciousness until now. And how many of them are relevant or needed today?"

If you like any of my questions, they're yours for the taking.

EPILOGUE

As I finish my *Memories and Confessions*, I am in my eighty-seventh year. People tell me "That's not old," and I tell them, "Nor is it young."

As I have grown older I have thought more about relocating to the Big Television Studio in the sky. I am an orphan; I am a gay man; I have only a loose relationship with a first cousin and her daughter on my mother's side and no one on my father's side. So I made a few decisions:

- I donate my body to the School of Medicine at the University of New Mexico for medical uses after which it should be cremated and the ashes scattered over water by Eric.
- I request there be no funeral. I am optimistic that my friends will say goodbye and remember me in their own private way.
- I bequeath everything I own to my friend, John Eric Roybal.

- I'm grateful that music was such an important part of my life—not as a performer but as an integral part of my being.

I lovingly remember Agnes de Mille. She was a woman of accomplishment and she became a late-in-life friend. I directed a video biography of Agnes at the end of which she wrote and spoke:

"Old age is an odd state, a condition of continual diminishing. Activities are curbed. Physical perceptions are lessened. Friends die one by one. But so, thank God, do enemies. In plain words, one doesn't care so intensely and whether this is good or bad, I cannot say. Certainly it does not engender intense activity and it would not do for young people to know this tranquility. But older ones are permitted to experience it and ought to."

Thank you, Agnes and bless you.

ATTACHMENTS

DANCE IN AMERICA PROJECTS

If I have been cavalier about the chronology of *Dance in America*, I include here a list of the ballets from 1976 through 1984, the years I directed. I have indicated which programs I directed and which ones were directed by others.

1976
Joffrey Ballet (Jerry Schnur)
Twyla Tharp: *Sue's Leg* (Merrill Brockway—[MLB])
Martha Graham Dance Company (MLB)
Pennsylvania Ballet (MLB)
American Ballet Theatre (MLB)

1977
Merce Cunningham: *An Event for Television* (MLB)
Dance Theatre of Harlem (MLB)
Pilobolus Dance Theatre (MLB)
Trailblazers of Modern Dance (Emile Ardolino—[EA])
Choreography by Balanchine—Part 1 (MLB)
Choreography by Balanchine—Part 2 (MLB)

1978
Paul Taylor Dance Company (EA)
San Francisco Ballet: *Romeo and Juliet* (MLB)
Choreography by Balanchine—Part 3 (MLB)

1979
Choreography by Balanchine—Part 4 (EA)
The Feld Ballet (EA)
Martha Graham Dance Company: *Clytemnestra* (MLB)

1980
Two Duets: Choreography by Jerome Robbins and Peter Martins (EA)
Katherine Dunham: *Divine Drumbeats* (MLB)
Beyond the Mainstream (MLB)
The American Dance Festival: Pilobolus Dance Theatre (EA)

I ended my association in 1980 with *Dance in America*, but in the following years I directed, as freelance assignments, the following:

1983
The Magic Flute with the NYCB

1984
San Francisco Ballet: *A Song for Dead Warriors*
A Choreographer's Notebook: Stravinsky Piano Ballets by Peter Martins
Balanchine, Parts 1 and 2, a biography

1987
Agnes, the Indomitable de Mille

1989
La Sylphide
Stella Adler: Awake and Dream!

1990
American Indian Dance Theater: *Finding the Circle*

New York: 1962—1993

The following is a printed chronicle of Merrill's broadcasts and projects principally in New York. He called it 'Biography of Merrill Brockway' in lieu of a resume when one was requested.

eginning in 1953 in Philadelphia and after 1962 in New York, Brockway produced and directed films and video for CBS Television—news programs, talk shows, sports events, children's programs, jazz and rock shows, symphony concerts, commercials and arts programs. From 1968 he served as Producer/Director of *Camera 3*, the CBS Television series that proposed "a stroll through the marketplace of ideas" and whose content ranged widely in the arts. In 1971 he was appointed its Executive Director. During this adventure Brockway produced and directed programs with Pierre Boulez and the New York Philharmonic, Alicia de Larrocha, Beverly Sills, the Living Theater, the Open Theater, the National Theatre of the Deaf, Japan's Classical Bunraku Puppet

Theater, the Royal Shakespeare Company, Peter Brook's Company, Maurice Bejart and the Ballet of the 20th Century, the Ritual Athletes of Iran and the Dancers of Bali—among others.

While he was with CBS, Brockway's programs received two Emmy Awards, two Ohio State Awards, a Christopher Award and an American Film Festival Award. In 1975 the Library for the Performing Arts at Lincoln Center sponsored a retrospective of his work.

Brockway joined PBS as Series Producer for *Dance in America*, where he directed programs with Twyla Tharp and Dancers, the Martha Graham Company, the Pennsylvania Ballet, American Ballet Theatre, Merce Cunningham and Company, Dance Theatre of Harlem, Pilobolus Dance Theatre, the San Francisco Ballet, the New York City Ballet in *Choreography by Balanchine*—Parts 1, 2 and 3. In 1979, *Dance in America* was awarded an Emmy for *Choreography by Balanchine*—Part 4, (Directed by friend and colleague, Emile Ardolino; produced by Brockway) and a Golden Hugo at the Chicago International Dance Festival for direction of Martha Graham's *Clytemnestra*. Earlier in 1979, Brockway directed the filming of the classic Kabuki drama, *Terakoya*, at the Kabukiza, Tokyo.

In 1980 Brockway joined CBS CABLE as Executive Producer of Arts Programming. He served as Executive Producer/Director of Balanchine's *Davidsbündlertänze*, with the New York City Ballet; *Kennedy's Children*, with Jane Alexander, Brad Dourif and Shirley Knight recreating her Tony Award-winning role for television; Elizabeth Swados' short opera, *A Tune, a Dream, a Letter* and *Sizwibanzi is Dead*, by Athol Fugard and performed by the Tony Award-winning cast. Brockway was Executive Producer of Twyla Tharp's *Confessions of a Cornermaker*, which won a 1982 Ace Award for innovative cable programming; *Resurrection of Lady Lester*; Pat Carroll's *Gertrude Stein, Gertrude Stein, Gertrude Stein*; May O'Donnell's *Dance Energies*; *Chamber Music Society of Lincoln Center*—Parts 1 *and* 2 and *Pilobolus on Broadway*. Brockway was also Executive Producer/Director of *Paris, I Love You*, with Zizi Jeanmaire and Roland Petit's Ballet National de Marseilles, which was videotaped in Paris, September 1982.

During 1983 Merrill Brockway:

- Directed for *Dance in America*: The New York City Ballet in Peter Martins' *Magic Flute*; The San Francisco Ballet in Michael Smuin's *A Song for Dead Warriors*.
- Toured China as a member of the Directors Guild of America group invited by the China Film Association.
- Was invited to visit Australia as a consultant for The Australian Ballet.
- Prepared a television proposal for six one-hour episodes of *The Life and Songs of Colette*.

During 1984 Merrill Brockway:

- Directed for *Dance in America: Balanchine*, a 2-hour television tribute to the work of George Balanchine.
- Was awarded an Emmy for direction of *A Song for Dead Warriors*.

During 1985 Merrill Brockway:

- Was nominated for a Directors Guild Award for *Balanchine*.
- Directed a commissioned-video celebrating Carnegie Hall.
- Began preparation for production in 1986 of five one hour Phil Donahue/NBC nighttime specials on the subject of the human animal.

During 1986 Merrill Brockway:

- Produced and directed for NBC: *Love and Sex*, the first episode of *Phil Donahue Examines the Human Animal*.

During 1987 Merrill Brockway:

- Directed for *Dance in America: Agnes, the Indomitable de Mille*, a video biography, which was awarded a 1987 Emmy for Outstanding Informational Special.
- Directed for *Great Performances: On the Move*, a performance documentary about The Central Ballet of China and its 1986 tour of America. This program received the Blue Ribbon Award from the 1987 American Film and Video Festival.

During 1988 Merrill Brockway:

- Directed for *Dance in America*: Peter Martins' staging of Bournonville's *La Sylphide*, with the Pennsylvania-Milwaukee Ballet in performance from the Academy of Music, Philadelphia.
- Was given a Directors Guild of America Award for *On the Move: The Central Ballet of China*.

During 1989 Merrill Brockway:

- Directed for *American Masters: Stella Adler: Awake and Dream!*, a video profile of a great theater legend.
- Directed for *Dance in America: Finding the Circle*, with the American Indian Dance Theatre.

During 1990 Merrill Brockway:

- Directed for Les Ballets de Monte-Carlo: *Celebration in Monte-Carlo*.
- Was nominated for a Directors Guild Award for *Stella Adler: Awake and Dream!*

From 1991 through 1994 Merrill Brockway:

- Was Coordinating Producer for the film *George Balanchine's The Nutcracker* with The New York City Ballet.
- Continued preparation for a film biography of Tennessee Williams begun in 1987, produced in 1993 and released in 1994 as *Tennessee Williams: Orpheus of the American Stage*.
- Completed video production and off-line editing of *Essays in the Balanchine Style*. Begun in 1985, this archival project of Balanchine's technique was planned to be nine 45-minute episodes. Since then three additional hours have been recorded.

Brockway has been a member of the Special Projects and the Dance Panels for the National Endowment for the Arts and is included in *Who's Who* and *Who's Who in Entertainment*.

The Beginning of What Would Be "The System"

FACT: We were transferring dances from the stage to television

FACT: The geometry is different:

- The stage is a rectangle
- Television is a triangle
- Ergo: a re-interpretation is called for

PROCEDURE/ SEQUENCE:

1A. Select a piece for recording and make a record tape for learning. This preserves the dancers' energy.

1B. Divide the piece into, no more than, five-minute sections; rehearse and record it that way. You don't want to go back to the top after every mistake, do you?

2. The director prepares: analyzes, explores the shot possibilities of each camera and prepares shot

sheets. We used three cameras; within a five-minute section, each camera has several assignments. If more shots are needed, repeat the section with new assignments, therefore, six cameras. Never forget the choreographer's intention, which the director learned through prior conversations.

3. The rehearsal is about the dancers: Retraining them from their usual 8PM performance mindset to one of a 9AM class and 11AM rehearsal and record section (in costume); then rehearse and tape, rehearse and tape, etc.

4. Camera Conference with cameramen and record tape from 9 to 11AM.

5. The recording studio is about getting the job done. The studio is expensive, *ergo*: no arguing, or no differences of opinion about subjects that should have already been discussed. Additionally, no improvising and no fooling around.

These guidelines are about protecting the dancers and informing the crew, listening to the choreographer and keeping people with opinions and suggestions off the director's back.

MERRILL'S TRAVELS

For a boy who had rarely been out of northern Indiana for the first twenty years of his life I discovered a roaring appetite for travel. The army kicked it off: Georgia, New York City, Colorado; then northern France, Belgium, Holland and Germany, not to forget rest leaves at southern coastal France, Switzerland and the Scottish Highlands.

My first civilian travel, during the Philadelphia period, was visiting London, Paris, Copenhagen and southern France (where anti-American passion was overflowing: I was shouted out of a restaurant by a raging waitress), Spain (where I first felt the mysterious power of the bullfight) and northern Italy (where I was hooked, especially by Florence).

The following year I, with a friend, drove from Barcelona through the Costa Brava to Marseille; then along the French and Italian Rivieras (driving only two hours a day in order to enjoy the beaches) to Genoa and, finally, north to Milan.

Another year the drive was from Lisbon south, through the Algarve to Seville and surrounding towns. Some of these cities and places I would visit again and several of them, again and again.

During the thirty-plus years in New York "The project", usually in some stage of production, determined the possibility of travel—unless travel was included in the assignment to direct film or video, such as:

- Brussels, Belgium (Maurice Bejart's *Nijinsky, Clown of God*);
- Tokyo, Japan (*Secrets of Kabuki*);
- Haiti (*Divine Drumbeats: Katherine Dunham*);
- Guanajuato, Mexico (*Ballet's Romantic Era*);
- Paris, France (Roland Petit's Ballet de Marseille):
- Monte-Carlo and Locarno, Switzerland (The Ballet de Monte-Carlo);
- Melbourne, Australia (as video consultant to the Australian Ballet in Melbourne, I was able to include side trips to Sydney and the Great Barrier Reef);
- Rapallo, Italy and Salisbury, England (for interviews with Gore Vidal and Lady Saint Just for *Tennessee Williams: Orpheus of the American Stage*).

Independent periods of travel that I negotiated with "The Project" were:

- Bayreuth (Boulez conducting Wagner's "*The Ring*". This was my first foray into Germany since the war—it was troubling; old memories wouldn't stay stored. My tip: "Don't go to Bayreuth for the cuisine," but the Festival was the last year of Boulez' *Ring* performances and the music was unforgettable) followed by safaris in Tanzania and Kenya with side visits to the Seychelle Islands and Mombassa; then Cairo and a Nile sailing (where I was surprised by members of the Martha Graham Company on holiday during a tour of Europe) to Luxor and Abu Simbel; the Galapagos Islands; then Quito, Ecuador (before a flat-boat sail down an Amazon tributary); on to the Iguacu Falls in Paraguay and finally Rio de Janeiro and Machu Picchu in Peru. I advise: "Always stay over night; the sunrise is wondrous."

- Northern India, arranged by editor, friend and native Indian, Girish Bhargava, guiding a group of his friends to Bombay, the Taj Mahal (a man was overheard saying, "I am getting drunk on its beauty."); Benares (getting up in the dark of night to drive to the holy Ganges to greet the sunrise); Nepal (dancing on New Year's Eve to dawn in Katmandu) and Delhi. As the group was leaving, the three Sikh killers of Indira Ghandi were sentenced to death. Driving to the airport the city was eerily quiet and the prime minister's house, then occupied by Indira's son, was under tightest security, fearing reprisals from the Sikhs.
- A Directors Guild of America tour of China: Beijing (sunless skies, an overflow of bicycles and the Forbidden City); Shanghai (one of the world's great seaports) and X'ian (home of the excavated terracotta soldiers) and, of course, the incomparable Great Wall.

Different single Mexico trips:

- Mexico City, Puerto Vallarta, the Yucatan and Guadalajara.

www.ingramcontent.com/pod-product-compliance
Lightning Source LLC
Chambersburg PA
CBHW031254090426
42742CB00007B/447